contents

illustrations 7
about the author 9
introduction 11
enjoy your hobby safely 13
    general health and safety 13
    food safety 13
    personal hygiene / cleaning 14
    separation 14
    cooking 15
    chilling 15
    storage 15
    safety with knives 16
    fire safety 16
    wood dust and chips 17
    footnote 17
the history of smoking and curing food 19
basic cures and brines 25
    how salt cures meat and fish 25
    cures 26
    brines and brining 28
    nitrite salts 29
    making brine 32
    chilling brine 32
    brining kippers 33
    adding flavours and sweeteners 33
the two main types of food smoking 35
    cold smoking 35
    hot smoking 36
sourcing wood 39
    foraging for your own 39
    wood from the internet 40
    preparation for smoking 40
combustion 45
    the triangle of fire 45
    definition of combustion 46
    pyrolysis 50
    what is smoke? 51
    combustion dynamics 52
    polycyclic-aromatic hydrocarbons (PAHs) 53
creating smoke from your wood 55
    factors to consider 55

type of wood	55
moisture content	56
size of wood shavings/chips	57
burning method	58
generating smoke	62
the cold smoke generator	63
the Venturi principle smoke generator	65
foil package smoke generator	69
the chimney effect	71
buoyancy	71
damper	73
heat	74
the smoke spreader	79
cardboard food smoker	83
getting started	84
using the cardboard smoker	87
the damper	89
loading the smoker	90
advantages of using the cardboard smoker	91
garden food smoker	93
smoker sides	96
smoker back panel	97
smoker door and front assembly	99
door and front detail	100
roof frame assembly	101
floor and smoke spreader assembly	102
assembling the side, back, floor and smoke spreader	104
side assembly	106
door furniture	107
fitting the rack supporting dowels	107
the smoke generator	109
improvised hot smoker	113
roasting tray method	113
Cameron stovetop smoker	115
barbeque grill hot smoker	116
hot smoked trout	117
smoking fruits, nuts, vegetables and cheese	119
smoked fruit	119
smoked tomatoes	120
smoked nuts	121
smoked peppers and chillies	122
smoked garlic	122
smoked paprika	123
smoked olives	123
smoked oils	123
smoked rice, wheat, lentils, beans and pulses	124

food smoking

a practical guide

Turan T. Turan

LILI

Published in October 2013 by

Low-Impact Living Initiative
Redfield Community,
Winslow, Bucks MK18 3LZ UK
+44 (0)1296 714184

lili@lowimpact.org
www.lowimpact.org

Copyright © 2013 Turan T. Turan

ISBN: 978-0-9566751-7-0

Design and Layout: Commercial Campaigns Ltd

Printed in Great Britain by:
Lightning Source UK Ltd, Milton Keynes

    smoked tofu 124
    smoked cheese 125
smoked salmon 127
    key steps to making smoked salmon 128
    things to consider 128
    purchasing the fish 130
    knives 131
    filleting 132
    pin boning 135
    salt curing 136
    dry salt cure 137
    brining 139
    drying 140
    smoking 140
    hot smoking 141
    cold smoking 141
    product storage 142
    slicing your very own smoked salmon 142
smoking meat 145
    smoked beef fillet 146
    hot smoked chicken 147
    smoked duck 148
    smoked venison 149
    smoked lamb 149
    pastrami 150
    spicy smoked beef jerky 152
smoked salt 155
    moisture 155
    cardboard 155
appendix a: nitrite concentration in dry cure mixes 157
appendix b: brining tables 159
appendix c: brine recipes 161
appendix d: summary of differences between smoking methods 163
appendix e: dos and don'ts when sourcing and processing wood 165
appendix f: burning characteristics 167
appendix g: smoke spreader design 169
appendix h: food hygiene guidance 171
    colour-coded boards 171
    general chopping board hygiene 171
appendix i: temperature conversion table 173
appendix j: characteristics of wood for food smoking................175
resources 179
    smoker suppliers and manufacturers 179
    information 181
    books 183

illustrations

fig 1: brine strength table (SAL degrees) 30
fig 2: brine strength graph 31
fig 3: the triangle of fire 46
fig 4: radiated heat affecting pyrolysis 47
fig 5: combustion of hydrogen and oxygen 49
fig 6: pyrolysis and combustion of wood dust 50
fig 7: supported smouldering utilising a draught 60
fig 8: indirect heating through a metal plate 60
fig 9: direct heating on charcoal 62
fig 10: ProQ smoke generator 63
fig 11: smoke dust large burn tray 64
fig 12: ProQ smoke generator loaded with wood dust 65
fig 13: the Venturi effect simplified 66
fig 14: steel can Venturi smoke generator 67
fig 15: steel can Venturi smoke generator lighting hole 67
fig 16: steel can Venturi smoke generator side view 68
fig 17: steel can Venturi smoke generator cross section 68
fig 18: aluminium foil smoke generator 70
fig 19: an example of a smoker using a remote smoke pipe 72
fig 20: the relationship between damper setting,
        heat and smoke production 73
fig 21: regulating the heat by extending the smoke pipe 76
fig 22: the effect of the smoke spreader 80
fig 23: smoke spreader design 81
fig 24: cardboard box 83
fig 25: cardboard box layout for marking holes 84
fig 26: cardboard box with access flap 85
fig 27: cardboard box smoker with dowels in place 86
fig 28: the garden food smoker 94
fig 29: the smoker sides 96
fig 30: the smoker back panel assembly 97
fig 31: the smoker door and front assembly 98
fig 32: the smoker door and front detail 99
fig 33: the smoker roof frame assembly 101
fig 34: the smoker floor and smoker spreader assembly 103
fig 35: the smoker back and side assembly 104
fig 36: the smoker side assembly 105
fig 37: the smoker assembly door catch details 106
fig 38: the smoker supporting dowels 107
fig 39: the smoker supporting racks 108
fig 40: the smoker high level dowel location 109

fig 41: the smoker remote smoke generator 110
fig 42: the smoker sawdust basket 110
fig 43: the smoker remote smoke pipe 111
fig 44: improvised roasting tray hot smoker 114
fig 45: Cameron mini smoker 115
fig 46: Cameron mini smoker with lid 116
fig 47: charcoal barbeque adapted for hot smoke 117
fig 48: salmon 131
fig 49: basic salmon anatomy 132
fig 50: filleting the salmon 133
fig 51: removing the first fillet 133
fig 52: removing the second fillet 134
fig 53: removing the ribs from the fillet 135
fig 54: pin boning the salmon fillet 136
fig 55: slicing salmon – the initial cut 143
fig 56: slicing the salmon – subsequent cuts 143

about the author

Turan is passionate about smoked food and has been smoking his own for over a decade. Brought up in West London in a family of caterers and restaurateurs he has had a close association with good food all his life. With parents from Cyprus and England his culinary palate has enjoyed some of the best food the Mediterranean and British cuisine has to offer. Although Turan has been surrounded by restaurateurs, his own career has taken him in a completely different direction; he serves as a career firefighter. As a serving firefighter for the last 29 years Turan still responds to emergency incidents in a senior officer role and enjoys the variety, excitement and challenges managing large emergency incidents brings. The irony of being a firefighter and someone passionate about smoked food is not lost on him – as he regularly reminds people it doesn't matter what job he's on, he still comes home smelling of smoke. Turan's fire service career has been a varied one serving as a firefighter and junior officer at many West London fire stations as well as in training and in various headquarters roles up to borough commander. Turan is also an active member of the Institution of Fire Engineers (IFE) contributing towards and promoting education in the science of fire. Turan serves on the IFE's fire safety examination and marking committee.

Turan's passion for smoked food has been primarily fuelled by his father's quest for good quality, affordable smoked salmon, a challenge keenly taken up by Turan and one which led to the design and building of numerous home smokers and hours of experimental curing and smoking. Successful in his quest for excellent smoked salmon Turan set up his website to promote home smokers and offer tips and advice online to those wanting to pursue this artisan craft for themselves. This passion for all things smoked lead to Turan's involvement with the Low-impact Living Initiative (LILI) when he stepped in at the last minute to run their food smoking course back in 2010. Since then Turan has continued his association with LILI in conjunction with his own regular food smoking courses which he hosts in London and all over the country. Turan has published articles for the Great British Food magazine and is a regular contributor on food related social media. Turan (52) has two daughters and lives in Milton Keynes, Buckinghamshire with his partner Alison. He operates his website www.coldsmoking.co.uk and www.smokedust.co.uk which offer equipment and resources for others keen on home food smoking.

introduction

Thank you for purchasing my book on food smoking. I have enjoyed smoking my own food for many years. The desire to smoke food was mainly driven by having a father who was completely immersed in the restaurant and catering business for more than forty years and someone who's pursuit for good smoked salmon seemed at times endless and often fruitless. I might say that having an innate interest in all foods from a very early age helped too: obviously the latter being cultivated by the former. Having the privilege of exposure to fine smoked salmon and fine cheeses at the age of ten and with regular encounters during family holidays with some of the finest Mediterranean food, I regularly found myself looking for ways to challenge my palate. Like many people I just love the flavour that a little wood smoke can give to what would otherwise be quite ordinary but good food. That's not to say you're going to turn a sow's ear into a silk purse by tickling it with smoke but if you get it right you'll definitely be turning good food into great food and opening up a wonderful field of culinary delights.

Whilst this book focuses on the mechanics of cold smoking food, building a smoker, and the theory behind food smoking, there is an important underlying message throughout the book about the way we produce and consume food. It's worth remembering that apart from adding another flavour dimension to your food, smoking food was originally used by our ancestors as a means of preserving back in the days before refrigeration. I think it's important to remember we can still rely partly on some of these methods instead of having to rely on ever more expensive energy to keep our food edible. There is great satisfaction to be had in food smoking especially where its impact on the environment is as low as possible. Underpinning this ethos is my unashamed desire to spend as little money as possible whilst achieving the best possible results. This book demonstrates that you can use a variety of inexpensive items and everyday objects to achieve the same if not better results than some of the best smokehouses on the planet. I also believe there is a kind of visceral satisfaction in producing your own smoked food that perhaps makes it taste a little better.

Whilst I like to keep things reasonably simple, I do like to go into some detail where I feel it's appropriate and of course where you the reader would benefit from a richer understanding of the subject matter. I hope I've managed to strike the right balance in this book which could have been a lot longer had it not been for this compromise. Within its covers I will be explaining the basics of cold and hot smoking; I will delve into the principles of combustion and will touch on the subject of brining and dry salt curing; I outline how to source your wood for smoking and I provide plans to build your own cold smoker and smoke generators, hoping you will build your own cold smoker and smoke your own food.

Little is known about the true origins of food smoking. There are few if any clues left from our ancient ancestors' attempts at smoking their own food. What we do know has mainly come from archaeological discoveries around the world. The ancient Egyptians were using salt and plant extracts to preserve food as long as three thousand years ago and many civilisations across the globe have used similar processes to extend the life of their foods. They say that necessity is the mother of invention and food preservation is a great illustration of this.

Well, not having a complete view into the past one could be forgiven for believing smoking food is a little like alchemy. When I first started curing and cold smoking my own food it all seemed a little bit daunting. Trial and error were the order of the day and some of my attempts to cure and smoke my own produce were completely unsatisfactory. I guess that's not completely unsurprising since there are so many variables to consider. It's also worth mentioning that some of my early results were incredibly successful and it's these successes that I want to share with you. It's typical that for the most part, the simple approaches to food smoking produce the best results, as is true for so many other areas of life.

My search for knowledge in this field has been a long and sometimes confusing one. When it comes to curing food you can find as many methods in books and on the internet as there are different foods. The same goes for exposing your food to wood smoke. My approach throughout this book is to simplify and demystify the process of smoking food and to give you ideas to take away and try for yourself. This is not a traditional 'How to' book, rather a practical guide to helping you on your way to building your own smoker and producing your own wonderful smoked food in a sustainable, eco-friendly way. My aim is to hand you the basics and then let you loose to experiment for yourself. Give someone a plate of smoked food and they'll enjoy it for as long as it lasts. Give someone a smoker and they'll enjoy smoked food for ever. Hopefully this book will whet your appetite and motivate you to embark on this fascinating and engaging pastime. In these days where the mere mention of smoking is frowned upon I'm not ashamed to wish you good luck and happy smoking.

Turan

enjoy your hobby safely

general health and safety

Health and safety is clearly very important especially when dealing with food preparation and handling sharp objects like knives and hot and dangerous things like fire and smoke… This chapter covers some of the basic common sense precautions to take to ensure you are operating in a safe and secure way so you won't get hurt while preparing or smoking your food and moreover your actions don't cause harm to anyone else.

food safety

There is a wealth of information about food safety on the internet and depending on your country's laws, the government usually takes responsibility for providing information and guidance on how to stay safe when handling and preparing food for your own or others consumption. There are comprehensive resources online to guide you through the finer points of food safety. The information I have included in this chapter is based around guidance commonly used in the UK and US but it's worth noting this information and guidance is by and large universal in its nature as it's based on a set of easy to follow rules backed up by a healthy portion of good old common sense.

In the US they follow a simple yet effective approach of Clean, Separate, Cook and Chill to ensure food is safe to eat. This aligns closely with the approach in the UK which adopts the approach set out in government guidance entitled *Safer food, better business (SFBB)*, see *resources*, page 179.

In the UK the four Cs of Cross-contamination, Cleaning, Chilling and Cooking are detailed in this guide issued by the Food Standards Agency and essentially spell out the same message as in the US – that provided you maintain your awareness and understanding of food hygiene and food safety issues and guidance so that

- you prevent your cooked or prepared food from becoming contaminated by raw ingredients
- you, your hands and surfaces are kept clean

- you keep raw ingredients at a low temperature
- you cook things thoroughly,

you'll be hard pressed to go astray.

Much of the guidance is aimed at food businesses where there is an assumption you will be providing food for consumption by the public but the information is just as useful for personal use at home and especially when smoking food for friends and family.

personal hygiene / cleaning

Personal Hygiene and cleaning is very important and it almost goes without saying that washing your hands before handling and preparing food is essential in preventing contamination. Wearing the correct clothing is important not just to protect the food from you but also to protect you from the food so your clothing doesn't become a vehicle for cross-contamination. Wear an apron or other protective clothing appropriate to what you are doing. Care should be taken not to touch your face before handling food and to always wash your hands after taking a break or going to the toilet. Smoking tobacco should not be allowed in areas where food is being prepared or cooked. (Except wood smoking of course)…!

Working on clean surfaces and ensuring surfaces are clean after use is also very important especially when handling high risk ingredients like raw fish and meat. Surfaces should be washed down with a recognised anti-bacterial disinfectant and rinsed with clean water before drying. Failing to do this simple yet effective step can lead to cross-contamination.

separation

Keeping raw and cooked foods separate is a key part of food safety. Separating raw ingredients from cooked food is important as raw foodstuffs like meat or fish may well have bacteria on their surface which, if not rendered safe through cooking, could be harmful to health if it comes into contact with cooked food through careless storage or poor hygiene. Usually when smoking food these rules apply to the raw ingredients i.e. when handling raw meat and fish before curing. Much of the bacteria on the surface of meat and fish will be rendered safe through the addition of salt during the curing phase but it's vitally important to maintain low temperatures when handling raw ingredients or ingredients that are in the process of being cured just to ensure they stay safe to eat. Keeping fish cold is particularly important as it has a tendency to spoil quickly if left at ambient temperatures.

cooking

Cooking raw meat and fish is generally accepted as a method for rendering them safe to eat provided their internal temperature is sufficiently high for a time to kill any harmful bacteria. It is generally accepted that food should reach at least 70°C for two minutes to render it safe to eat. When hot smoking raw ingredients it's likely these temperatures will be achieved but it's always worth checking the temperature with a probe to confirm this, see *resources* page 179.

chilling

Chilling food, especially high risk foods like raw meat and fish, is particularly important to prevent bacterial growth. It is recommended that chilling is important while curing fish or meat and after curing whilst drying before smoking. Most commercial smokehouses are temperature controlled where high risk products are involved. This is something that the amateur smoker will struggle to achieve unless they convert an old fridge to a smoker. Maintaining a low temperature whilst cold smoking salmon and raw meat can be difficult in some climates; I tend to aim for a temperature well below 30°C if I can achieve it. For longer smoking times it is advisable to keep a keen eye on the temperature to make sure it is not going to exceed the maximum (30°C). To achieve a low temperature in the smoker I have on occasion smoked at night. Sometimes during a cool day direct sunlight on the smoker can lead to excessive temperatures and it becomes necessary to place your smoker in the shade. When I run food smoking courses I tend to operate the smoker under the shade of a gazebo to protect the smoker from unwanted solar radiation.

storage

When you've finished smoking your food it's always advisable to refrigerate it to extend its shelf life. There are some cost-effective vacuum sealing machines on the market these days which can, if used correctly, extend the shelf life of your smoked food by months. Vacuum packaging your smoked food prevents freezer burn and ensures the condition of your smoked food is maintained.

safety with knives

When using knives always ensure your knife is sharp. When making cuts try whenever possible to cut away from your body and always keep your hand behind the edge of the knife. It is well known that a blunt knife is more dangerous than a sharp one because one has to use a great deal more force to cut with a blunt knife than with a sharp one and therefore the chance of slipping or sudden movement is greater. Food smokers will be no strangers to a kitchen knife and will use them to fillet and prepare meats, fish and cheese for the smoker. Never rush when using a knife and take your time when making cuts. Always place your knives in a safe and secure place so that they don't become a danger to yourself and others later.

fire safety

It may seem a little obvious to some that basic fire safety measures are a given when food smoking but I still get asked regularly if it is possible to smoke food indoors. If you are a commercial smokehouse with a proper procedure for ducting and temperature control then it may be possible to operate indoors. For the vast majority of amateur smokers this will be an outdoor pursuit kept well away from the house to prevent the spread of fire should the unexpected happen. Using the correct equipment properly and following all the relevant guidance should keep you on the straight and narrow but never take any chances with fire – it can get out of control very quickly and it won't be long before you'll need professional intervention to extinguish your mistake.

To summarise: never smoke food indoors unless you are using a dedicated stovetop food smoker under a suitable and sufficient smoke or fume extractor. Always ensure your outdoor smoker is situated in an open space separated from other structures to prevent fire spread should the worst happen.

It may seem a little counter-intuitive to suggest not exposing oneself to smoke when it's OK to eat smoked food. Obviously we are going to eat our smoked food but smoke itself is a respiratory irritant and can cause severe discomfort. Smoke residue on the food we've smoked is OK in moderation but do remember smoke contains a number of different and complex chemical compounds so smoked food should not really be consumed in excessive quantities to avoid ingesting too many of these compounds, some of which can be hazardous to health in high concentrations over a long time.

wood dust and chips

Wood dust and chips can cause respiratory irritation if the airborne particles are inhaled. Be careful when working with wood dust especially as this can liberate quite high levels of airborne particles when bagging up or re-charging your smoker. Make sure you have a dust mask or other suitable respiratory protection to hand when undertaking these activities.

footnote

As a health and safety practitioner in my main career I am constantly amazed at the use of health and safety by some people as an excuse not to do something when in fact health and safety is there so you can continue to do your chosen activity time and time again safely without injuring yourself or others. Health and safety needs to be seen as an enabler to doing things safely for the long term and not as a preventative measure. The only thing health and safety is there to prevent are accidents – not activities. OK enough said!

the history of smoking and curing food

We know from ancient archaeological sites around the world that salt was at one time a very precious commodity both for culinary and preservation purposes. It has been known since the beginning of time that salt is a major requirement in our diet and indeed is essential in many ways for life itself. The magical properties salt holds are still being used today, every day and in every corner of the globe to perform culinary alchemy in so many ways. Smoking food too has been a central part of our food heritage as a species for millennia. Drifting back through the mists of time to a people who were predominantly hunter gatherers we first discovered fire and mastered the art of using it as a tool to our advantage; to heat us, assist us in hunting, to provide light for us when it was dark, to signal to others and to cook our food. There is little evidence in the archaeological records to support the theory that smoking our food goes back to ancient times but it would equally be naïve to suggest otherwise. It would be naïve to suggest food smoking is something new in our food culture and history. One sensible theory for the lack of evidence could lean towards the fact that smoked food was as popular then as it is now and therefore all the evidence had been eaten. OK maybe not that sensible, I may be joking but I bet there is a sliver of truth in that theory.

Let's imagine for a moment we can go back in time, back to a time when we were a primitive species. Imagine our needs as a people, perhaps working together as a tribe, a social people. We may well have hunted together, eaten together, lived together and supported each other in our unending pursuit of nutrition. Perhaps we would have even starved together in lean times when we weren't that successful. As we developed we mastered the art of making our food last into the lean times. This was a key skill to develop as we would have had no means of refrigerating our food in temperate climes and the meat we caught would have gone off quickly without protection. Very basic methods of making food last longer were mainly driven by the prevailing climate. Freezing food in cold climates and drying food in more temperate regions. As we developed as a species, it's likely our first attempts at preserving food was with evaporated sea water or concentrated sea water brines. As far as smoking food is concerned it's likely we used to hang our meat in the smoke to prevent flies attacking the meat and causing it to spoil. Now it's easy to accept this as a deliberate act but it's more probable that our original intention was to hang the meat high up in our dwelling, whether this was a cave or shelter, to prevent it being eaten by scavengers. It's not too much of a stretch of the imagination to suggest that smoke from the fires we lit to keep ourselves warm drifted up to the meat hanging high in the cave or shelter to inadvertently at first bathe our meat in wood smoke. We learnt that insects and bees have an instinctive and almost reflex action towards smoke or, I should say, away from smoke and this is something shared by many other creatures. This obvious fact would not have escaped the notice of primitive man and would have been widely used to protect and preserve food for later use. Although it's likely that our first smoked meats were 'happy accidents' it wouldn't have taken very long for our ancestors to learn that the properties of the smoke applied to their foods made it last longer. It wasn't until much later that scientific discoveries and advancements in chemistry revealed there are certain compounds within smoke that have natural anti-bacterial and anti-microbial properties.

Virtually all human development has been the result of a series of steady, logical, incremental steps, slowly developing knowledge, understanding and skills. Learning from mistakes and moving on by handing this hard-earned knowledge down from generation to generation. It's a lovely thought that food smoking and curing is nothing more than a convoluted series of happy accidents which kept our food fresher for longer, sustaining our civilisation whilst at the same time pleasing our palates with an aromatic smoky flavour and of course allowing us to thrive as a species. Quaint notion perhaps, but it's these steps which provide us with the most rational and plausible explanation we have to explain the use of smoke and salt as preservatives.

Even in Iron Age communities there is some evidence to suggest food was hung indoors high up in the centre of the roundhouse out of reach of ground dwelling insects, scavengers and coincidentally and conveniently hung above the fire. It's probably fair to include drying in the list of preservation methods too as this would have undoubtedly assisted in the preservation process and is certainly true for hotter climates where the use of fire to heat dwellings was not so commonplace. We can surmise, I think quite accurately, that the logical steps we've taken, and the discoveries we've made out of necessity along the way have no doubt added to our rich food heritage. Our taste for slightly salty, smoked food is one that has been with us for millennia and one which has been refined over many centuries to give us the broad range of cured, dried and smoked food we enjoy across the world today. It's incredible to think that smoked, cured or dried food in one form or another forms part of almost every food culture on the planet and this is certainly not an accident.

The rich herring stocks from the North Atlantic and the North Sea provided a healthy bounty of protein for the people of northern Europe and North America. Before the days of refrigeration these fish would have been dry salted or brined to preserve them. These methods of preservation together with smoking are still common today and are particularly popular in the countries bordering the North Sea and North Atlantic regions. It's interesting to note that in persistently warmer climates there appears to be fewer if any indigenous examples of smoked foods when compared to colder parts of the world. Although in many warm regions of the world cooking with wood over open fires is common, this method only imparts a smoky flavour as part of the overall cooking process and is really a crude form of the hot smoking process we use. Drying meat high above open wood fires would have naturally given the meat a smoky flavour over time and there is evidence from hunter gatherer tribes that this was a common method of preserving the food for extended periods of time. Native Americans and Dutch settlers in South Africa have used this method of food preservation to good effect in producing cured and dried meats from various animals resulting in products like beef jerky and biltong. There are few examples in India and Saharan Africa of smoke being used as part of the native food culture to add preservation and flavour to cured or raw foods. One possible reason to support this observation may be that in order to preserve food in hotter climates using the power of the sun to dry or desiccate food by reducing its moisture content is logical and much simpler than using other methods like smoking, brining or salting and the effect in prolonging its life is pretty much the same. One argument to support this hypothesis could be that in warmer climes the use of wood fires as a source of home heating would be rarer and one could argue that the chances of the smoke having the opportunity to impart a flavour on the food would be less.

In temperate regions which experience seasonal weather, a variety of different methods have been adopted to suite the prevailing conditions.

This is reflected in colder climates like the UK and North America where the warmth from fire serves a strong purpose in our very survival and has been used to good effect in both drying and smoking food for preservation. The wide variety of smoked, brined and pickled products may well have some strange association with the weather which would have undoubtedly affected the local conditions favouring one method over another.

One can travel through the Middle East, India and into the Far East and not come across the same prevalence of smoked food as we are used to in the west. This is not to say you won't find food smoking going on in parts of the Far East. There are some fine examples of tea smoked duck and fish in regions of China where the use of tea to smoke food is common. It is worth mentioning though that the method used to smoke with tea is used as an adjunct to the cooking process to enhance the flavour and was in no way intended to preserve the food in the way salmon or kippers are smoked in the West. Smoking food with tea is usually done in a wok over a heat source with either a wire rack and foil or a bamboo steamer and lid, mixing the tea leaves with uncooked rice is one method used to generate the smoke but there are examples where tea is used on its own.

In the west, and in particular Europe, smoked food, whilst commonplace, holds a special place across cultures and attracts high prices when compared to their unsmoked equivalents: German smoked sausage, cheese, hams, the Arbroath Smokie, bloaters, kippers, fine smoked salmon, ducks, venison and many other fine meats. Vegetables also enjoy substantial improvement from the addition of smoke and Spanish smoked chilli (Chipotle), smoked paprika and, more recently, speciality smoked olive oils are no stranger to the palate. Smoked shellfish like mussels and scallops are truly delicious and the difference smoke can make to nuts like almonds and cashews is truly sublime. All things considered, whilst this ancient art was once a necessity for our very survival as a species, we've managed to hang onto it even in the face of modern methods of food preservation and if nothing else this demonstrates our passion and love for the flavours smoke brings to our palate. Even sweets can benefit from the addition of smoke and a fine example of this is smoked raisin fudge. Admittedly my invention but clearly illustrating the point that we are in some respects only limited in our endeavours by our imagination.

The skills associated with what can best be described these days as an artisan craft, are known only to a select few producers, hobbyists and adventurous chefs who have taken the time and effort to add them to their repertoire. What a wonderful string to one's bow. I can't think why any self-respecting chef or gourmet cook wouldn't want to either pursue their goal or maintain the wonderful art of turning good food into great food with just the addition of smoke. As you start on your own personal quest in pursuit of this food alchemy take a moment to reflect on the fact that somewhere back along our lineage we have an ancestor who would have been practising food smoking routinely probably not even aware of the significance of what they were doing. It's true that over the years and particularly since the second world war we have seen the decimation of our fishing fleets across the UK and in particular in Grimsby and along the east coast where the air used to be thick with the aroma of fish and smoke and where now only a few boats and smokehouses ply their trade. With the mechanisation of many processes and the changes in our diets brought about by the advent of fast food it's easy to see how skills like food smoking, curing and drying could quite literally drift into the mists of time to be forgotten by the many only to be preserved by the few. Well hurrah for the few for keeping it going to the point where we now view smoked food as a premium product when it used to be a staple for many families. It's interesting to note that in recent times there has been a real resurgence in the interest in food provenance and slow food which is a truly great thing for us all. Getting in touch with our food heritage, learning and practising these skills is surely the best way to pay homage to all those food smokers past and present who have kept this fascinating process alive, it's in our very DNA. I salute you.

basic cures and brines

Some may argue that a book on food smoking should really be focusing on food smoking and not on salting and brining. To do so, I think, would be to miss a huge trick. From my perspective the process of food smoking has to start with some form of preparation for the food you are about to smoke. Not with all foods I grant you, but for the vast majority of food you're going to smoke like fish, fowl and red meats you will want to cure or season with salt beforehand. The application of a curing agent, whether it's dry salt or a brine solution, is an important process which will undoubtedly affect the finished product. There are lots of books on the market covering the subject of brining and preserving food and there are a host of resources on the internet with recipes to follow. This book is not trying to teach you how to brine and cure, rather to give you an insight into the key principles and practices as I feel they are important if you are then going to go on to smoke your food.

Salt is an extremely precious commodity and has been so since ancient times. The Romans used to pay their armies in salt (hence the word salary comes from the Latin for salt (*sal*) and silver (*argentum*) which was used for monetary purposes, and thus effectively 'salt money'). Curing or preserving food with salt has been practiced for thousands of years that we know about and probably a lot further back in time, beyond where we have any tangible records.

how salt cures meat and fish

The transformation meat or fish undergoes with the application of salt through salting or brining is nothing short of miraculous. Salt reacts with meat and fish by liberating moisture from its cellular structure which in turn makes for a difficult environment for bacteria to thrive. Bacteria need the right conditions in order to multiply successfully and without sufficient water bacteria find it extremely difficult to proliferate, add salt's chemistry into the equation which also doesn't provide a good place for bacteria to grow at all and you have the fundamental idea behind salt curing.

Salt cures meat and fish in two ways, firstly by absorbing moisture from the surface of the flesh simply through direct absorption which initially creates a very concentrated brine solution as it mixes with the moisture from the flesh and then through a process called osmosis at a cellular level. Osmosis in simple terms is the movement of solution with low solute (salt in solution) content through the semi-permeable cell membrane in an attempt to maintain solution equilibrium on both sides of the cell wall. This process effectively reduces the moisture level in the cells of the flesh as it attempts to move low solute solution through the semi-permeable cell wall. The moisture in the cells of the meat or fish passes from the cell through the semi-permeable cell wall and into the relatively high salt concentrate solution of the brine. This reduction in moisture firms up the flesh and assists in preventing the growth of bacteria. The process is enhanced by salt's innate ability to prevent bacterial growth.

Reducing the water content of the flesh salt also enhances and intensifies the flavour of the meat or fish.

OK that's about as technical as I'm going to get for now. I'm not going to use this book to delve too deeply into the chemistry and physics behind curing as that's the subject of a whole book in itself. I can't say the same for the smoking process as we will cover that in depth later in the book.

cures

When I refer to cures I mean dry cures, which is essentially dry salt applied to the surface of either meat or fish.

Typically this is the traditional method for salt curing salmon when producing smoked salmon. Salt is simply hand sprinkled onto the flesh of the boned and trimmed fillet and allowed to stand for a period of time before being rinsed off and dried in preparation for the application of smoke. Dry salting in this way is one of the simplest methods to adopt to achieve an acceptable cure. In some curing houses the salmon is laid out on inclined boards before the salt is applied to allow excess moisture from the curing process to drain away. This serves to prevent over curing in its own salt by preventing the fillet from laying in a concentrated brine solution formed by the moisture as it is leached from the fillet. Dry salting or dry curing as it is sometimes called will generally produce a dryer, firmer cured meat then immersion in brine. But this is largely dependent on the curing time.

There is a debate about which type of salt is the best to use or which one is more effective for dry salt curing. There are many types of salt on the market: sea salt, fine granular table salt, pure vacuum dried (PVD) salt to name a few. I like to be able to control the amount of salt I apply to meat or fish and aim to adjust the amount of salt I use in proportion to the thickness of the fillet or cut of meat being cured. I tend to use less salt on the thinner parts like the tail end of the salmon and more salt towards the thickest part of the fillet towards the gill plates. This method attempts to cure evenly across the whole cut of meat or fish and in my experience is easiest to achieve by using fine granular salt. I have seen some smoked salmon producers using sea salt which has a much larger flake and takes longer to cure the flesh. I would urge the novice to try both methods to see which one suits their taste. I have tried both methods and achieved great results. This is one area where it's mainly down to personal choice.

One note of caution when curing is to avoid using lo salt products or iodised salts as these tend to contain salt substitutes like potassium chloride and are not good for what we want to achieve. They are fine for seasoning your food but not for curing.

It is possible of course to add ingredients into the cure to introduce flavour and sweetness to whatever it is you are curing. Sugar, and many other herbs and spices, can be added to the dry cure to enhance flavour but remember it's the salt that does the curing and must form the majority of any cure mixture you apply to whatever you are curing.

I have devoted a whole chapter of this book to the production of smoked salmon, see page 127, so it only seems appropriate to describe the method I use to cure the salmon here. The cure I use couldn't be simpler; for the basic cure I use just plain salt. Some suggest only using sea salt but I find that using free flowing fine granular salt allows for a much more even coating on the salmon. Sprinkle a small amount of salt into the bottom of a non-metallic dish and place a fillet of salmon skin side down on top of the salt. Gently sprinkle salt onto the fillet lightly covering it with a very thin layer of salt. Allow for this layer of salt to absorb some of the surface moisture from the salmon and then apply another, similar quantity of salt to the fillet. The layers of salt should be slightly translucent so one can still just see the salmon colour below the salt. Take care to adjust the thickness of the salt in proportion to the thickness of the fillet. So that the thicker part of the fish receives slightly more salt than the thinner parts. This is important to ensure an even cure throughout the fillet.

It must be remembered that this is a basic cure, without additional flavourings, and can be applied to an average tail end fillet of salmon for four to six hours. The salmon can then be washed, dried and smoked to your taste.

brines and brining

Brine in its simplest form is water and salt and is sometimes known as a wet cure or immersion brine, cover brine or cover pickle.

Brining is an immersion technique using a solution of salt dissolved into water. The finished product tends to retain higher water content than dry cured meat or fish and is not a good method to use ahead of cold smoking as you really want to achieve a greater degree of drying as part of the cold smoking process, with the obvious exception of kippers, haddock and other cold smoked fish which are brined before cold smoking. More about that later.

Brining fulfils two basic functions, firstly it cures the flesh increasing its preservation properties and secondly and, some would say, more importantly it can provide an opportunity to add a variety of flavours to the meat or fish you are curing. Brine curing could fill a book by itself; there is an almost infinite variety of flavouring ingredients that can be used in curing brines. It's not unusual to use herbs, sugars, spices and alcohols to impart character to food. For the purposes of this book I will just touch on the subject of brines and will include a few recipes later in this chapter to whet your appetite.

Brining is usually undertaken before smoking and is used as more of a preservative in products like kippers and haddock. Arbroath Smokies, on the other hand, are brined to enhance the flavour of the fish. My basic brine is always the same strength. Maintaining consistent brine strength is helpful because through your experimentation you will be able to replicate your brining with some degree of accuracy. In addition to this benefit, if you feel your finished product is too salty, rather than varying the brine strength you can adjust the time in the brine. My preferred brine strength is 80 per cent (SAL). Please see the following *classifications* section for more detail. Many recipes call for different strengths for the brine so having access to the brining table and strength graph, figs 1 and 2, can aid greatly in getting the brine strength right.

nitrite salts

Using nitrites and nitrates as part of the process of curing is important when protecting against bacterial growth. Although the main function of salt in curing is to prevent the development of bacteria, not all bacteria are killed by salt alone. The nitrite's main function is to prevent botulism which is a highly toxic bacterium capable of growing in very low levels of oxygen. Because botulism is so toxic it is advised to use nitrite or nitrate salts as part of the curing process as they are effective in killing this pathogen.

In years gone by the limits on the use of nitrates and nitrites in food was a lot less stringent than they are today. Along with salt, there are established health issues related to a high intake of nitrite and nitrates in food products. To address these health issues there are closely monitored limits on the use of nitrates and nitrites in cured meat products and throughout the world governments have set out limits on their use. The aim of the legislation is to strike a balance between the need to take account of the health risk from the use of nitrates and nitrites while maintaining microbiological safety. In Europe the EC have set out limits for the use of nitrates and nitrites in meat products at 150mg/kg. This is the same ratio as 150 parts per million (ppm). The limit for sterilised meat is lower at 100mg/kg. or 100ppm.

classifications

Brines can be broadly classified into three bands: heavy, medium and light.

- Heavy Salt Brine: between 70 per cent and 100 per cent (SAL degrees)
- Medium Salt Brine: fall between 40per cent and 69 per cent (SAL degrees)
- Light Salt Brine: between 10 per cent and 39 per cent (SAL degrees)

Brines below about 15 per cent SAL degrees are too weak to be really effective for curing as they would take far too long to act.

The percentage rating I use for brines is based on the maximum amount of salt that can be dissolved completely into a given volume of water. This measurement is called Salometer degrees or SAL. It can be seen from fig 1 that 100 per cent brine based on the SAL degree measurement will be 357.8 grams of salt in one litre of water at around 15°C.

Salometer Degrees	% of Salt by Weight (Baume Degrees)	Gms of Salt per Litre of Water	Gms of Salt per Litre of Brine
0	0.0	0.0	0.0
5	1.3	13.3	13.3
10	2.6	27.1	26.8
15	4.0	41.1	40.6
20	5.3	55.6	54.6
25	6.6	70.5	69.0
30	7.9	85.8	83.6
35	9.2	101.6	98.5
40	10.6	117.8	113.6
45	11.9	134.6	128.9
50	13.2	151.7	144.6
55	14.5	169.4	160.6
60	15.8	187.8	176.7
65	17.2	206.7	193.2
70	18.5	226.1	210.1
75	19.8	246.4	227.1
80	21.1	267.1	244.4
85	22.4	288.7	262.2
90	23.8	310.9	280.2
95	25.1	334.0	298.5
100	26.4	357.8	317.2

fig 1: brine strength table (SAL degrees)

Some books on brining and curing will express the brine strength as a percentage of the weight of salt in a given quantity of water, so one litre of water (1000g) with 100g of salt dissolved into it would be expressed as 10 per cent brine. This method of measuring brine strength is known as Baume degrees (B°). Antoine Baume was an 18th century pharmacist who developed this scale to measure the density of different liquids and it is based on weight. My preference is for the Salometer degrees scale or SAL as it is known as it can be expressed across a range from 0 to 100 whereas the Baume scale can only go from 0 per cent up to a maximum of 26.4 per cent. This is because it is not possible to have a brine of greater strength than that as the salt concentration would be too strong for all the salt to be held in solution.

Having two different methods of measurement can cause some confusion especially if you are unclear which units or scale you're using. In the example above some would say the brine is 10 per cent brine while others who measure brine strength using the SAL scale would classify this brine as approximately 40 per cent brine strength.

To give you an idea how strong brine can be it's worth comparing the strength of sea water with the light brine that we use for preparing our food before smoking. Sea water is approximately 4 per cent brine based on the Baume degree scale so it only has around 4 per cent by weight for a given weight of water. This is about 13.5 per cent on the SAL scale

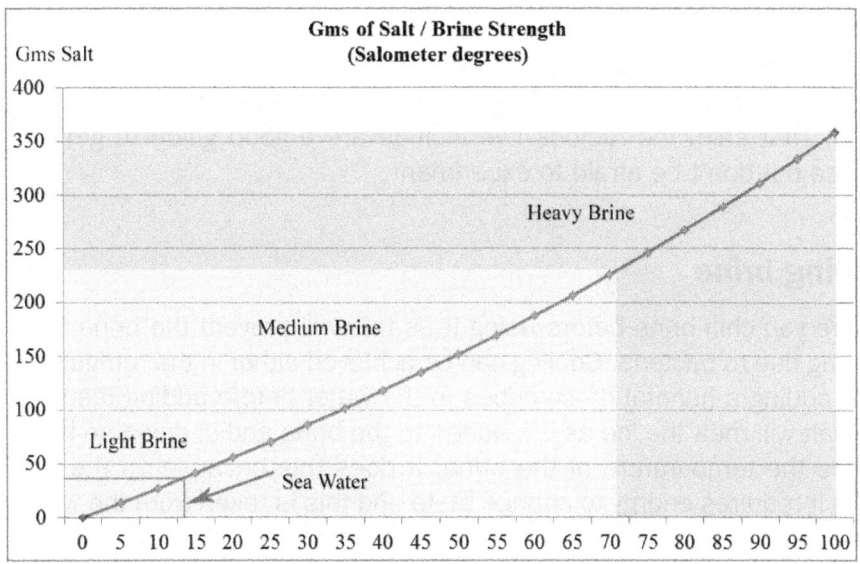

fig 2: brine strength graph

The two scales for measuring brines can be summarised as follows:

Baume degrees (B°) – Based on the percentage weight of salt to weight of water.
Salometer degrees (SAL) – Based on the percentage of the maximum amount of salt that can be dissolved into solution of a given quantity of water.

making brine

Making basic brine is very simple. Just dissolve salt into water to achieve your desired strength and away you go.

First make sure you have enough water to cover the food you are wishing to brine and refer to the strength table, fig 1, to get the right brine strength. When first starting out it's worth sticking with the same brine strength no matter which food you're brining. The reason for this is quite simple. If you maintain one constant it's possible to vary one other factor (like the time) to suit your taste for salt. This is useful to you when experimenting to achieve the right saltiness to suit your palate. I find that brining, while perfect for enhancing flavour in the food you're brining, is actually a very personal taste. Some palates are very sensitive to salt whereas some can take a lot. This subjectivity in taste renders most recommendations for brining times and strengths little more than a rough guide. That said, the recipes I've include are a good guide to get you started but don't be afraid to experiment.

chilling brine

Ensure you chill brine before using it as this will prevent the brine from spoiling due to bacteria. Cooling can be achieved either in the refrigerator or by adding a handful of ice cubes in the water before adding the salt. The salt will melt the ice as it's added to the brine and in doing so it will reduce the temperature of the brine. It does this because as the salt melts it requires energy to change state and this is taken from the water in the form of heat. This is a phenomenon known as latent heat and is sometimes used in some old fashioned ice cream makers to reduce temperatures to well below freezing point. It can be a very effective way of quickly reducing the brine temperatures.

If you do adopt this nifty scientific method of cooling your brine remember to take the volume of the ice into account when calculating the water you need so you maintain the correct finished brine strength. For instance, if you want to use 200ml of ice to assist in cooling the brine make sure you only add an additional 800ml of water to the mix otherwise you'll end up with the wrong brine strength.

brining kippers

Strictly speaking a kipper is not a kipper until it has been smoked so we'll refer to it as a herring for this paragraph. To turn a herring into a kipper, first you will need to brine a couple of back split herrings. Back splitting a herring is a simple knife technique for flattening out the herring keeping its belly cavity intact so it stays in one piece giving that familiar look. So, while supporting the fish dorsal fin uppermost on a chopping board and with your knife, working from the dorsal fin (top) cut the herring in half along its length towards the tail. Reverse the knife and continue splitting the herring along its back into its gut cavity continuing towards the head and cutting right through its head so it can flatten out, taking care not to cut all the way through the herring. Flatten out, remove the guts and gills and wash under cold running water, hey presto you're ready to brine.

I make brine with one litre of water in a non-metallic dish. To make kippers I use 80 per cent brine based on the Salometer scale (this is 267g salt to one litre of water). Slowly pour the salt into the water stirring constantly until it is completely dissolved into solution. Ensure the brine is chilled to below 4°C before immersing the split herrings in it. The herrings should be immersed completely in the brine solution for 20 to 30 minutes, removed, rinsed under running cold water, patted dry with kitchen towel and returned to the fridge to dry for about an hour or two before smoking. One can adopt a similar brining technique for brining hot smoked fish like an Arbroath Smokie which is, of course, a haddock fillet.

adding flavours and sweeteners

Sugars, herbs and pickling spices can also be added to give extra flavours to the finished brine. It is possible to add a variety of different flavourings to enhance or impart flavours into the food you're brining but it's worth noting that whilst sugar will add a hint of sweetness it has very little impact on the curing process itself other than to add flavour, and colour where caramelised sugars are used (with the exception of treacle or molasses). It's also reckoned that there is little discernible difference between the various types of sugar on the market when it comes to taste and also widely accepted that sugars in brine can have a masking effect on the saltiness of a brined piece of meat, so can be a welcome addition to a brine if you are intolerant of salt.

A good tip is to reduce the strength of your brine if you are adding flavours to it. The reason for this is that if you use a 'heavy' brine (like my standard 80 per cent brine) you wouldn't want to immerse your food in it for more than about forty minutes. This isn't really enough time for the additional flavours to infuse into whatever it is you are brining. Therefore a weaker brine solution allows more time in the brine so that more flavour can marinade the food.

If you are interested in producing your own brine recipe or would like some inspiration in assisting you to create your own brines I have included a few brine recipes which can be found in *appendix c* on page 161.

the two main types of food smoking

There are two basic methods of smoking which are distinctly different from each other and should not be confused. The aim of both types of smoking is broadly the same in that you are imparting the wonderful taste and aroma of wood smoke into your food. The two methods of smoking are cold smoking and hot smoking and both methods of smoking will be covered in detail in this chapter.

cold smoking

Cold smoking is arguably the oldest form of food smoking and is achieved at low temperatures, usually well below 30°C. Cold smoking is traditionally seen as more of a preservation method which involves a two stage process of curing with salt then smoking. For obvious reasons this method of smoking was an important way of ensuring food availability during lean times and before the advent of mechanical means of refrigeration. It's worth noting here, cold smoking is not a cooking process so the food remains essentially raw, albeit cured, smoked and slightly dried. The salt in the cure and the smoke work hand in hand to ensure the food remains free from bacterial growth. Some of the many compounds in wood smoke act as a preservative on the surface of the food. Phenolic compounds like guaiacol which is formed from the combustion and decomposition of lignin contribute to the antibacterial properties of wood smoke. Essentially, the food coming from a cold smoker will be raw and will require further cooking with the obvious exemption of products like cold smoked salmon, cold smoked trout and smoked cheeses and nuts. Kippers and cold smoked haddock are good examples of cold smoked foods which require further cooking after smoking.

Because cold smoking is achieved at relatively low temperatures care must be taken to ensure the temperature remains well below the critical limit of 30°C. This can be problematic especially in climates where the ambient temperature approaches this limit. Cold smoking should not be attempted in weather conditions at or below freezing point (0°C) as the smoke will only condense on the surface having little or no penetration into the flesh and there will be almost no drying during the smoke application leading to a poor finished product.

Because cold smoking requires the application of 'cold smoke' well below the temperature of 30°C it is necessary to apply some level of control to either the way in which the smoke is generated, or how the smoke is transmitted to the smoker. It may seem a little obvious to state this but, as mentioned in the chapter on *combustion*, see page 45, combustion involves some level of heat which won't be helpful to the cold smoker. There are several arrangements for taking the heat out of the smoke and monitoring its temperature; whether this is done using a thermometer inside the smoking compartment or in some other location where the smoke is en route to the smoker is a matter of choice. The two main ideas behind controlling the temperature of the smoke are firstly to restrict the size and speed of combustion, which I will describe in more detail in the *combustion* chapter, see page 45, and secondly to transmit the smoke to the smoker in such a way that the heat from the smoke is allowed to dissipate to its surroundings mainly through conduction.

Although controlling the combustion process is very important when cold smoking, in a limited way the design of the smoker and its features can assist in controlling the combustion process and should not be excluded from the mix.

hot smoking

Hot smoking can best be described as a cooking process during which wood smoke simultaneously imparts flavour to the food. Albeit a very simplistic description it summarises the whole process quite succinctly.

It would be quite wrong to suggest hot smoking is the exclusive domain of the barbeque fraternity. There are many hot smoking processes like the manufacture of hot smoked mackerel, the Arbroath Smokie or smoked sausage which don't include the use of a barbeque. Hot smoking is a versatile method of cooking with smoke or smoke roasting. There are many dedicated hot smokers on the market ranging from stovetop hot smokers to dedicated multi-rack, digitally-controlled, commercial hot smokers. The major difference with these hot smokers when compared with cold smokers is they require the application of heat to not only generate smoke from the wood dust or chips but to cook the food as well. The temperature range for hot smoking can vary greatly from 75°C up to around 120°C. At these temperatures the food in the smoker will be ready to eat straight from the smoker or can be allowed to cool before consumption.

Whilst hot smoking is generally considered to be a single stage process, without the need for a salt cure, this is not always the case. Some country hams and smoke-roasted bacons will be cured in salt brine for days before receiving a hot smoking and the use of salt or brine before hot smoking is widely used in the production of hot smoked fish like Arbroath Smokies and hot smoked mackerel but this is more as a seasoning and flavour enhancement than for preserving the food.

sourcing wood

Sourcing wood to generate smoke can be a very easy and enjoyable pursuit. Most of the wood I've used in the past for this purpose was sourced locally from pruning or from generous tree surgeons off-loading a few choice logs. The best time for collecting wood for smoking is during the winter or very early in spring before the sap has had a chance to rise. The sap will add moisture to the wood and affect the smoke flavour as sap contains some complex sugar compounds. When these compounds are burnt to produce smoke they can impart a mild bitter note. This can be avoided simply by choosing when you cut your wood. Having said that, I have also had some great success with wood harvested during the summer but that's probably because I tend to go for a light touch when smoking food so I rarely achieve the concentrations of caramelised sugars that would result in a bitter note on the food. If I had a choice, I would go for the winter harvested wood every time.

foraging for your own

A few years ago I bumped into a tree surgeon and his gang of lads in a café on the A10 in north London. They had a load of fantastic oak logs on their truck which had just been cut down in one of the local municipal parks. I asked the gang leader if I could have a few logs and he was more than pleased to help. It didn't even cost me a cup of tea. These logs were in great condition without any disease. I simply took the ends off with a planer to discard any chainsaw oil residue that may have been present from when they felled the tree. I de-barked them, split and dried them for around four months and turned them into shavings using my electric hand planer. A word of advice about using wood that has been felled with a chainsaw; always take off a thin sliver of the wood from each end of the log as soon as you can. If this is left for a long time the chain oil can penetrate some way into the wood and you wouldn't want to be smoking with chain oil in your shavings, would you?

Once you know which woods you can and can't use it is great fun just looking around on your travels to see what you can pick up for free. You may have a suitable fruit tree in your back garden or a majestic oak or beech. No real need to head out into the garden with an axe and sacrifice the whole tree. It's amazing how many chippings you can harvest from a decent autumn pruning session.

In my early days of smoking I only remember buying wood once and that was a packet of hickory chips from the local DIY store. Hickory imparts a lovely strong flavour and it's always nice to have some of this wood around. It's a shame it doesn't grow in this country. I bought it to hot smoke some pork spare ribs in a kettle barbeque and I can say with authority that it was money well spent.

wood from the internet

You can see sellers from time to time on the web and on auction sites selling various wood shavings, chips and dust. These can be very useful especially if you have difficulty sourcing your own woods where you live or you simply don't have the time. Personally, I think there is a great deal of pleasure to be had from sourcing your own material for what is a wonderful and creative pastime. As I teach food smoking all over the country I only source and sell my dust and chippings from food grade sources. This is important and gives one assurance that the wood dust has been tested for heavy metals, is disease free and has been stored correctly.

It's a lovely idea to think the local joinery workshop making oak furniture will have an abundant stock of wood shavings and saw dust for your smoking. Although this sounds like an attractive prospect, especially if you have a local source, I would urge that you approach with caution; unless you can absolutely guarantee the source of wood shaving is what they say it is then leave it well alone. There are a lot of joiners these days using MDF and softwoods like pine and to have a batch of oak or cherry contaminated with either of these products will render any food you smoke inedible at best and perhaps quite dangerous.

preparation for smoking

If you've decided that you are going to make your own chippings or dust at least once, this section is for you. You're going to need to create chippings or dust if you're going to stand any chance of getting your wood to produce smoke when you light it. This isn't as difficult as it sounds, but there are a few things to bear in mind when you do it. Firstly, and even before we get to the stage of making chippings, your wood will have been cut.

How your wood is cut down has some relevance to how you'll proceed with processing it to a point where you can use it to smoke food. If the wood has been cut with a hand saw, all well and good. You can get on with turning it into chips right away. However, if the wood has been cut down by a chainsaw you'll need to ensure any remaining oil residue from the chainsaw's automatic chain lube system has been removed. This can be done by sawing a small disc from both ends using a hand saw or as mentioned earlier by taking a small amount from each end with a planer. The sooner this is done the better as chain oil can be drawn into the wood through capillary action.

Before going any further with the processing of your wood it's worth discussing the question of 'bark on' or 'bark off'? Well, it depends! If your chosen wood has a smooth bark like cherry or birch then it's perfectly possible to peel only a thin layer of the bark back to ensure you have a clean layer which has no contamination on its surface. It's fine to include the bark in the shavings or dust where they are smooth and easy to peel and you can guarantee they are clean. Bark acts to protect the tree and some are very thick with folds and crevices. Oak and Sweet chestnut are good examples of heavy bark. These kinds of bark can harbour all sorts of dirt, bugs and fungal spores and road grime. In my experience it's better to remove them from the wood before processing begins. Removing the bark also aids the drying process and allows you to see the young wood to check for disease. I find the easiest way to remove the bark is to do it while the wood is still green just after cutting and then using a screwdriver or other thin bladed object simply separate the bark from the wood. You'll find that it comes away quite easily. If the wood is allowed to dry with the bark on it can be a little more difficult to remove but you'll get there in the end if you persevere using the same technique.

OK, we have sourced the wood and we're ready to turn it into chippings or dust. Now, this is where I like to know what I'm going to use the wood for before I decide on how to process it. If I'm going to use it for hot smoking on the barbeque, then I'll more than likely chip the wood using a proprietary wood chipper (available from most hardware stores). Remember to follow all the safety instructions for the power tools you use. I always wear the correct PPE (Personal Protective Equipment) eye, hearing and respiratory protection when generating chippings or shavings as these tools can make a lot of noise and dust. If you're processing a log you will be running these tools for some considerable time. Wood chips are medium-sized pieces about half a centimetre square. These chippings can be used on a barbeque after soaking the chips in water for about two hours. The chips can be placed directly onto hot charcoal to produce smoke. As they are larger and denser than wood shavings, they'll take longer to combust than shavings or dust.

I have used my own electrical garden chipper to produce pear, apple, cherry, bay and oak chips and dust and it's an excellent way to collect your own smoking woods especially if you are fortunate enough to have a wide selection of trees, shrubs and herbs at your fingertips. Do make sure that before using your garden chipper you take the time to give it a really good clean to get rid of any unwanted garden rubbish that has built up inside it.

If I'm going to use my wood for cold smoking I'll generally go for dust as it smoulders far more reliably than shavings and doesn't generate much heat while smouldering. The *combustion* chapter, see page 45, covers the smouldering characteristics of different grades of wood (chips, dust and shavings). Please also see *appendix f*, page 167, for fuel sizes and their various burning characteristics.

I use an electric planer connected to a dedicated industrial vacuum cleaner to collect the mass of shavings that can be generated from one log. The size of the shavings can be adjusted by changing the depth of the planer's blade. It works really well and I get perfect fine shavings every time.

The by-product of creating fine shavings is dust which can be sieved from the shavings with a garden sieve or other coarse mesh grid. In commercial operations dust is generated as a by-product of the chipping process. Typically for every ton of chips produced in a commercial environment, approximately 50kg of this will come out as dust and will be collected and sold separately from the chips.

Using a planer to produce shavings will also produce as by-product, a quantity of dust which will be well mixed in with the shavings. The total output from the planer will generate a mass of shavings which will contain about 85 per cent shavings and 15 per cent dust. This method actually produces considerably more dust than the chipping process and therefore I tend to use my planer to produce dust for cold smoking as I have a basket smoke generator which uses shavings. It's also quite therapeutic turning a large oak log into shavings and dust using an electric planer.

Once I have all the shavings in one place I put them into an open bag for a few days to further dry out to around 16 per cent moisture content and then place them in a sealed plastic bag to maintain their condition. Allowing the shavings to dry out any further can lead to them catching fire when they are lit in the smoker. This is not such a problem for dust as it is for shavings as the dust will tend to maintain a continuous smoulder and not burst into flames. Don't be tempted to store your dust or shavings in a sealed bag straight from the planing process as the excess moisture will eventually turn your lovely wood shavings into compost. A very good compost but expensive all the same.

While we are discussing wood dust it's worth remembering that inhaling wood dust can damage your respiratory health and should be avoided at all times. During the manufacturing process of shavings, chippings and dust it's inevitable that you will come into contact with airborne dust particles so I always recommend wearing a dust mask to prevent inhaling them, as they can be a severe acute irritant for some people and the chronic effects are not very good either.

Producing large quantities of shavings or chippings with your electrical hand tools or domestic garden machinery is very likely to invalidate any warranty these tools have. The quantity of wood you're likely to put through these machines is going to cause blades to wear out. To minimise the effects of blade wear, it's worth shaving or chipping the wood when it's not completely dry as the wood will generally harden as it dries out. The sooner this is done after cutting the wood, the better. Just remember that when you've chipped or created shavings from green wood this will need to be allowed to dry out in an airy environment. *appendix e*, page 165, has some handy tips on what to do and not do when sourcing and processing woods for food smoking.

combustion

the triangle of fire

The triangle of fire is a very simple representation of the relationship between the different elements which go to make up the combustion process. For combustion to take place it is generally accepted that three elements must be present. These elements are fuel, heat and oxygen. I mention that the triangle of fire is a simple representation of the relationship between fuel, heat and oxygen because it deliberately leaves out time from the relationship. It could be argued that time is not really relevant in terms of combustion but it's worth mentioning it here because in almost every other explanation of the triangle of fire I have come across, time is left out. Its importance can be illustrated simply by representing the elements of the triangle with their respective parts.

So, oxygen will be drawn from that which is present in the atmosphere; the source of heat in this example will be a burning match and the fuel will be a tree trunk. All the elements for combustion are present and one can logically see that the tree trunk will eventually combust providing we imagine for this example we are using an everlasting match. The only factor not represented in this equation is time which I think you'll agree is after all an important factor in the combustion process. I will discuss the issue of time later in this chapter when I discuss the speed of combustion and how this affects smoke production. It can therefore be argued that a more complete pictorial representation of the combustion process could be made by representing it as a square. However, the whole purpose of the triangle of fire is to demonstrate the relationship between the main elements - fuel, heat and oxygen and how by removing one of these elements from the process, combustion will cease. This relationship is shown in fig 3 and is an important relationship for prospective food smokers to understand as it's the management or balance of these three elements which go into producing the smoke we will eventually use for food smoking.

In fig 3 all three elements of the triangle are in place and combustion will be sustained so long as the three elements are present. Take any one of the three away and combustion will cease. That said, our aim in food smoking is to maintain combustion under controlled conditions. Too much heat and there will be flames, lots of heat and very little smoke. Too much oxygen will produce rapid combustion too leading to lots of heat and eventually flaming combustion with little smoke. To achieve the 'goldilocks' combustion that's just right for smokers these three elements of the triangle need to be controlled and balanced. This is not too difficult to achieve with a little trial and error. It's worth noting that some forms of wood dust have a natural tendency to smoulder slowly in a reasonably stable and predictable way. This is helpful when we're using this kind of dust however when we want to use other types of chip or shaving, knowing how to set up the combustion process to control the fuel, oxygen and heat can be very useful indeed and makes the process of food smoking a whole lot more flexible.

All three elements must be present for combustion to take place

Take away any one of these elements and the combustion will cease

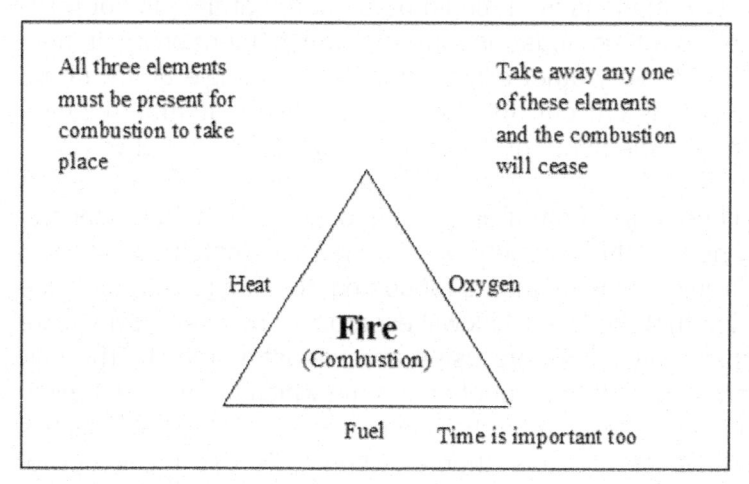

Heat   Oxygen

Fire
(Combustion)

Fuel   Time is important too

fig 3: the triangle of fire

definition of combustion

Combustion is essentially a self-sustaining, non-reversible chemical reaction between a substance most commonly known as a fuel and oxygen or an oxidising agent. This reaction between the fuel and oxygen releases heat and light and is known as an exothermic reaction. When we think of combustion we generally think of some sort of burning and when we think of burning we tend to think of flames. The type of combustion which involves the production of flames is unsurprisingly called flaming combustion. Flames are a very interesting part of the combustion process as they represent a particularly fast relation when compared to slower forms of combustion which don't involve flames, like smouldering.

Flames are usually present in the gaseous part of the fire where gases are produced and sustained by the heat from whatever is combusting (usually in the form of flames). Flames are a complex and rapid chemical reaction between the decomposing (due to heat) elements of whatever is burning and oxygen, which release a considerable amount of heat. When flames are present there will be large amounts of heat released which can be radiated back onto the surface of the fuel, decomposing or pyrolysing more fuel and producing more flammable gases which in turn sustain flames until the fuel or the oxygen is exhausted or when the heat is removed. That's the main mechanism for combustion to be regarded as self-sustaining.

Small Flame - Low levels of radiated heat - Low pyrolysis

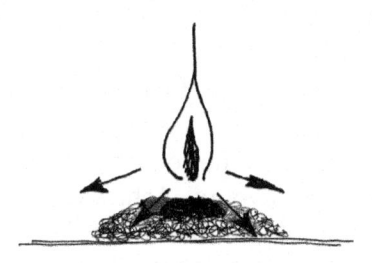

Medium Flame - Higher levels of radiated heat - Increasing pyrolysis

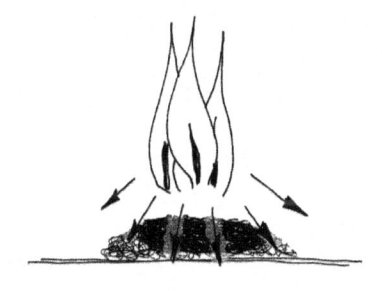

High Flame - Extreme levels of radiated heat - Rapid increase in Pyrolysis

fig 4: radiated heat affecting pyrolysis

However, whilst combustion requires the presence of oxygen it doesn't necessarily require a flame to be considered as self-sustaining. If you consider smouldering as an example, and this is the form of combustion which is particularly relevant to cold smoking, where the temperatures involved are approximately half those of flaming combustion and the speed of propagation through the fuel is much slower (by a factor of around ten or more) when compared to flaming combustion. We will discuss this more sedate form of combustion in more detail later in this chapter, see page 52.

Combustion in its most basic form can best be represented by the reaction between hydrogen and oxygen, which, when reacted together in a theoretically perfect mixture will form pure water (H_2O) and heat. The exact equation is $2H_2 + O_2 = 2H_2O$ + Heat. Remember that combustion is a one way chemical reaction that cannot be reversed. I've simplified the process here to demonstrate the point that what you put in, you get out, but in a different form and in changing from one thing to another, energy is either released as a consequence of the reaction or is required to assist in the reaction. In this instance energy is released in the combustion of oxygen and hydrogen into water. This example which demonstrates combustion is a very simple form of that process.

However, in food smoking where the fuel is wood, the chemical changes that occur in the combustion of wood are extremely complex. It is these complex molecules in the plume of smoke that gives smoke its characteristic aromas and flavours. Achieving perfect combustion is almost impossible outside of laboratory conditions which is something of a benefit for food smokers because it's the management of the combustion process which is the key to producing the smoke we need to smoke our food. Although the breakdown, decomposition and combustion of wood is in itself a complex one and outside the scope of this book, it is worth delving in a little further to consider some of the other factors in the combustion process.

There are usually other compounds formed during the combustion of carbonaceous materials such as carbon monoxide (CO) and carbon dioxide (CO_2). To further complicate matters, because there is 78 per cent nitrogen in the atmosphere we breathe, several forms of nitrogen compounds like nitrogen dioxide are also produced during the combustion process. I mention these compounds not because they affect the flavour or aroma, they don't, but because they are dangerous

fig 5: combustion of hydrogen and oxygen

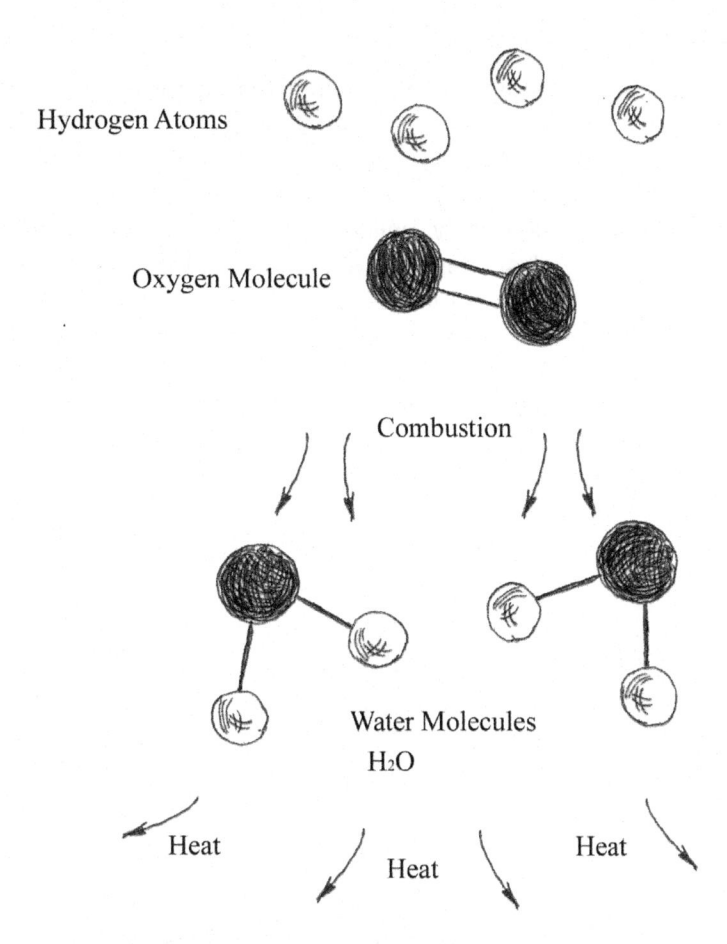

and reinforce the very strong message that, with the exception of a stovetop smoker under an efficient extractor fan, food smoking is primarily an outdoor pursuit. This may seem obvious to most but not everyone appreciates the dangers, especially from CO, and there have been several recent tragedies with portable barbeques where people have operated them indoors! CO is a colourless, odourless and flammable gas which has the ability to kill with just one breath if inhaled in a concentrated form. While in most cold smoking applications the production of CO is minimal, there are occasions when it may be advantageous to use charcoal as a means of supporting the combustion of wood and in this situation CO is likely to be produced in quantities that can cause significant harm if used in an enclosed space.

pyrolysis

We have discussed basic combustion principles so far but in terms of food smoking and the production of smoke there is another term used to describe smouldering which is distinctly different from the general term 'combustion'. Pyrolysis is the term used to describe the decomposition of a substance due to heat. Now, unlike combustion which requires the presence of oxygen, pyrolysis can take place without the need for oxygen as it just requires heat to decompose the substance being pyrolysed. If you imagine the process employed to produce charcoal this is largely achieved by using a sealed vessel called a charcoal kettle which utilises heat from the initial combustion of the wood that is being turned into charcoal to continue to pyrolyse the wood in a sealed, oxygen-deficient atmosphere to produce the finished charcoal.

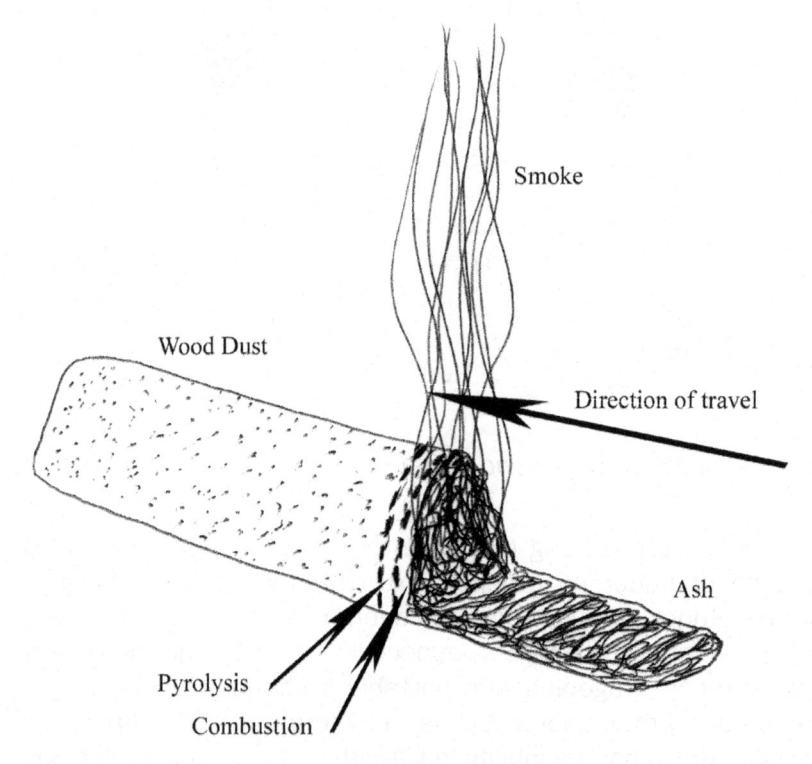

fig 6: pyrolysis and combustion of wood dust

Pyrolysis is also used in the indirect heating of wood dust or chips as is typical in a hot smoker where the heat pyrolysing the wood is provided by a stove or other indirect source without any direct contact between flame and wood. Pyrolysis is important from a food smoker's perspective because it produces lots of smoke at relatively low temperatures. When I say relatively low temperatures of course I'm comparing it with the temperatures associated with flaming combustion. Fig 6 shows the process of wood smouldering where the face of the wood dust is combusting which in turn, due mainly to the heat it is producing, pyrolyses the adjacent wood dust in a continuous process until all the fuel is exhausted.

what is smoke?

The decomposition or combustion of wood produces a number of complex chemicals which go towards making up what we generally refer to as smoke. The general term used to describe smoke for fire professionals is 'products of combustion'. I've already explained that pyrolysis and combustion are different processes and both produce smoke so the term 'products of combustion' is not really an accurate reflection as smoke could equally be described as the products of pyrolysis! Having said that, what's in a name eh? I will stick with the term 'products of combustion' as it describes the gaseous flammable chemicals produced from the decomposition of wood through heat.

The finer details of the decomposition of wood through heating is outside the scope of this book but for the curious amongst you I will dedicate a small amount of detail to this part of the food smoking process as after all it's the bit where it all begins.

To understand what smoke is it's worth knowing about the raw ingredients we intend to use to produce the smoke. The main constituents of wood are cellulose and hemicellulose, which account for around 60 per cent of its content, and lignin which accounts for around 20 per cent, the remainder is made up from sugar-related compounds and water. These percentages are average amounts and vary somewhat between tree species. When wood is heated, the molecules in these complex compounds become excited to the point where they eventually break away from their main structure, forming new compounds and molecules, some of which can be particularly volatile and nasty and are known as free radicals which are particularly reactive with other compounds. Within the smoke produced by this decomposition process there is a fair proportion of water, carbon dioxide, carbon monoxide and phenolic compounds which account for the aroma and flavours associated with smoked food. Having a basic understanding of this complex process is important because woods from different tree species have different ratios of cellulose, lignin and sugar-related compounds which influence aroma, flavour and rate of burn. Smoke is essentially a condensate made up of fine particulate matter, water, gases and chemicals derived from the burning wood and its interaction with atmospheric gases. The gases produced from combusting wood are flammable and if they form in sufficient concentrations with a suitable source of ignition they can ignite with the usual consequences.

Flaming combustion takes place in the gas phase of a substance, which is when the substance decomposes giving off flammable gases which become ignited to produce flames, whereas pyrolysis takes place on the surface of the fuel and in the case of food smoking this will be taking place on the surface of the sawdust without the presence of flames.

In reality we should be discussing pyrolysis before combustion as pyrolysis occurs before combustion takes place. The word pyrolysis comes from the Greek words pyr = fire and lysis = separate. When we generate smoke for cold smoking and hot smoking it's perfectly possible to use both processes.

combustion dynamics

In this context the dynamics of combustion refer to the speed at which the combustion process takes place. I briefly mentioned earlier that the speed of combustion is an important aspect in food smoking. This is especially important when you are cold smoking as temperature is an important factor.

When I use the term speed of combustion, what I am referring to can best be illustrated by comparing a burning match and a smouldering cigarette. The match burns a lot faster, releasing large quantities of heat in a short period of time whereas a cigarette is much slower burning, releasing heat at a greatly reduced rate at a significantly lower temperature. Weight for weight, dust that smoulders has essentially the same calorific value as match wood. Whilst the match wood will burn faster releasing its heat over a relatively short period of time, the dust will release the same quantity of heat over a longer period of time.

Due to the nature of different materials and their ability to absorb heat, the slower the heat is released from the food-smoking combustion process, the more time that heat has to dissipate and become absorbed by the food or the structure of the smoker and therefore there will be less chance of a situation where the temperature inside the smoker becomes a problem. Likewise, there are other combustion design controls that can be introduced to lower the speed of combustion and reduce the area where combustion takes place resulting in lower rates of heat release from the smouldering wood dust. These two factors are vitally important for cold smoking because the temperature is a critical element in the process. This balancing act is always going to be a compromise as there is always going to be a need to generate sufficient smoke to bathe your food to produce the desired taste.

polycyclic-aromatic hydrocarbons (PAHs)

Polycyclic aromatic hydrocarbons or PAHs are a major atmospheric pollutant originating predominantly from the burning of fossil fuels which also includes wood. PAHs range in toxicity from being quite benign to extremely toxic. Many PAHs are carcinogenic and there are several different categories in the group. The common link between all PAHs is their chemical make-up which includes the arrangement of two or more aromatic rings. Because we combust or pyrolyse wood to produce smoke it is inevitable that we will produce PAHs in various quantities. It's these compounds that contribute towards the flavour and aroma compounds in smoke and therefore their production is in a sense deliberate. For commercial smokers there are strict limits for PAHs in smoked foods and in April 2005 the European Commission introduced limits for benzo[a]pyrene (BaP) (which is one of the markers for indicating the presence of PAHs in food) in a range of foods, including smoked meat and smoked fish. This was published in Commission Regulation (EC) 208/2005.

Most smoked meat and fish have a limit of 30μg/kg wet weight which reduces to 12μg/kg wet weight from September 2014. The limit for BaP is 5μg/kg wet weight reducing to 2μg/kg. It's clear that as an amateur smoker one would not go to the trouble and expense of analysing samples of your food to check compliance. This is clearly impractical for most sensible people but there are some common sense measures one can adopt to limit one's exposure to these compounds. It is sensible not to consume smoked food every day. Little and often is going to be better for you. 'All things in moderation' is the key. Limit the exposure your food has to the smoke. This will naturally limit the amount of PAHs your food will be exposed to. It's worth noting that PAHs are more easily absorbed in oils than in water so oily smoked food is likely to contain more PAHs than those foods without. It's true to say that PAHs are more associated with grilled or barbecued food and higher in charcoal-grilled food than in gas-grilled food. There is also evidence to suggest that meats that are grilled further from the heat source contain lower levels of PAHs. For someone home smoking, PAHs are no more of a problem than if they were cooking food on their barbeque.

creating smoke from your wood

factors to consider

The production of smoke is the cornerstone of effective food smoking (no really!) and to achieve the best smoke you will need to take account of the following factors:

- type of wood
- moisture content
- particle size and shape (Size and shape of the wood - shavings, dust or chips.)
- combustion process

All these factors have a bearing on the production of smoke. Oak burns slowly while ash is a fast burning wood. Dry wood burns faster than green timber (the term given to freshly cut wood) and is more likely to catch fire than green wood or wood with higher moisture content. Shavings and sawdust are more likely to smoulder than chips which are more likely to self-extinguish unless there is sufficient heat or draught to sustain combustion. If too much airflow is present wood chips and shavings can catch fire easily. The same applies if too much heat is present. One could be mistaken for thinking producing smoked consistently is quite difficult but providing you understand a few basic principles and follow some simple rules you won't go too astray.

type of wood

Simply put, different types of wood impart different flavours to your food. Alder will give a delicate light smoke while hickory will give you a full-flavoured, rich, smoky flavour. Fruit woods are particularly popular and apple and cherry are my favourites. Some wild woods like hawthorn and blackthorn (sloe) are also very good for smoking and are similar in character to the fruit woods like apple and cherry albeit a little stronger. Each wood species has slightly different characteristics and will add character and colour to whatever you smoke. In *appendix j*, see page 175, there is a reasonably comprehensive list of wood varieties with their smoke and flavour characteristics. The list also provides information on which woods are traditionally used for certain foods.

moisture content

Moisture content in wood is an important factor in the combustion process. Although we may think the wood dust we use is dry, it can have around 16 per cent water content and still feel dry to the touch. Wood when it is cut is usually termed as 'green' and for our purposes, wood with a moisture content of more than 20 per cent water by mass will be termed as 'green'. Generally speaking, wood used for food smoking should be well below 20 per cent moisture content and usually below 16 per cent. This is not necessarily true in all cold smoking applications as there are some smokers that use damp sawdust in their smoking kilns, usually because there is a mechanically driven air supply and the moisture in the dust prevents a flare up. With the moisture content below 20 per cent there is little opportunity for the wood to deteriorate and it is likely to keep for a very long time. I've personally kept dried shavings for up to 3 years with no visible signs of deterioration.

Using wood straight after it has been cut while the sap is rising (i.e. in late spring or summer) can lead to a slightly bitter taste from the smoke. Just allow the wood to dry out so it can lose some of its moisture content before using it on the smoker. This will happen a lot quicker if you chip or shave the wood first so spread it out thinly on a baking sheet or other clean dry surface to allow it to dry out naturally before storing it away in a sealed bag. If you don't dry wood dust or shavings out before packaging you will end up with a bag of lovely compost.

The moisture content in your wood is very important for all forms of smoking because if your shavings or dust are too dry they are liable to flare up and if they are too damp they will not sustain a smoulder effectively when lit and will spoil in storage. Dry wood flare ups are more likely in shavings because they have more oxygen around them due to their shape and size and are typically thin and easy to ignite. If this happens, it is a good idea to lightly dampen the pile of shavings with a water spray from a hand held sprayer. You can get these from your local hardware store. However, if you there is too much moisture you will struggle to achieve the smouldering you desire. If wood shavings or dust are left open to the atmosphere they are likely to absorb moisture from the air which can have a marked effect on their smouldering performance. The reason for this is quite simple. The heat energy produced when wood dust smoulders heats the adjacent wood in a continuous process. If the wood contains high moisture content, a large amount of that heat energy used to maintain smouldering will be used up in raising the temperature of the moisture in the dust until it evaporates. When this happens there will be less heat energy available to continue the smouldering process and it is likely smouldering will cease. Water has a tendency to soak up a large amount of heat energy just in raising its temperature to boiling point and then a whole lot more to change its state from water into steam. This heat would have otherwise been used to sustain the smouldering process and as it's being used for something else, the heat energy in the smoulder will drop and combustion will probably cease.

I have on occasion been faced with a situation where I cannot get my wood dust to smoulder. This is more often than not because the bag of dust has been left open to the air and attracted too much moisture. If I suspect my wood dust to be moisture rich I usually place it on a metal baking tray and pop it in the oven at 120°C for around ten to fifteen minutes, just to allow any moisture to be driven off. Don't do this if you have a gas oven. Pop the dust back in your smoking tray and give it a go. I find that in the vast majority of cases where my dust fails to smoulder it's largely due to moisture content.

size of wood shavings/chips

The size of the wood used for generating smoke is significant in terms of the various methods which can be employed to generate smoke for food smoking. Fine particles have a tendency to smoulder, which is a quality not shared by coarse wood chips. As a general rule of thumb different forms of wood chips, dust or shavings can be used for different food smoking applications. While this is true in most cases, it is possible with the right techniques and equipment to generate smoke from shavings, chips or dust for use in either hot or cold smoking applications. Stating this may sound a little contradictory but to enjoy this level of flexibility you will need to use more equipment and if you take that approach the whole ethos of using less resources and minimising the impact to the environment would more than likely be lost. The section on chips and dust, see page 60, looks more closely at the choices of material for hot and cold smoking.

As a general rule, wood shavings have a tendency to smoulder really well all by themselves providing they aren't too dry and they have just the right balance of air flow; chips smoulder less well as they have a lower surface area to weight ratio and therefore need the added heat energy from an outside source like a charcoal barbeque or other heat source or an adequate air flow to maintain combustion. To illustrate this point, imagine setting fire to a large log by using the flame from a match. The log has a very low surface area to weight ratio and therefore the available oxygen to support combustion around its surface will be lower. Add to this the sheer mass of the log and it's clear to see that the log will absorb the applied heat which again will take the heat energy away from supporting the combustion process. It will be very difficult to set alight and burn. Now turn the same log into sawdust. The surface area of the dust will be huge and the available oxygen around the surface will be infinitely more abundant. The dust will burn and smoulder readily from the same heat source.

The analogy of the log is interesting because there are some circumstances when a log will continue to smoulder if it has sufficient air flow to maintain and support combustion. This is demonstrated in some of the smoke generators which use an air supply to maintain combustion. I discuss these smoke generators later in this chapter.

burning method

The burning method, as I term it, can be very important. By burning method I mean how you physically burn the wood. There are four methods that categorise the way in which we can generate smoke from wood. These are:

- unassisted smouldering
- supported smouldering
- indirect heating
- direct heating

unassisted smouldering

In my cold smoker for instance I use a tall, thin, wire-mesh basket to hold the shavings in a column. I light this on the top using a blow torch and allow the shavings to burn down to the base of the basket. This unassisted smouldering method seems to work well because the diameter of the basket (20cm) limits the cross-sectional area of the shavings allowing only a finite area of smouldering combustion at any one time. This is particularly useful in cold smoking as heat produced during combustion can be a problem. Slow burning wood with a limited area for combustion will give a longer, cooler burn using this method. In addition to this, I have found that compacting the shavings slightly in the basket gives a slower more even smoulder. The up side of this is that the temperature of the smoke is generally lower and of course, I'm able to add more shavings for a given basket size which extends the time I can smoke for. Controlling the air supply to the shavings is also important as this is a key part of the relationship in the triangle of fire, see page 45.

There is a need to balance this relationship and sitting the basket of shavings inside a container which has some method of controlling or restricting the air supply can be of great benefit in managing this process. We will discuss this control mechanism in a little more detail when we discuss the purpose of a damper as a means of controlling the combustion process, see page 73.

By piling the shavings into a natural cone shape, you can have them burn from the tip of the cone down and outwards to the periphery of the base. This can work if your smoke generator has a wide flat base. The only problem with this method is that you have very little control over the combustion process unless you limit the supply of oxygen to the fire. This method of combusting wood could lead to a situation where there is a large area of smouldering with copious amounts of smoke being produced, for a relatively short period of time. This method is OK if all you are aiming to do is to lightly smoke some produce. One disadvantage of this method is the potential for heat build-up leading to a potential flare up. This is really where controlling the combustion process comes down to restricting the flow of air to the wood and can be achieved simply by the use of a damper. When a flare up happens, the products of combustion (the smoke) actually catch fire and all the constituents of the smoke that impart flavour to your food will be burnt in the combustion process.

supported smouldering

Supported smouldering is a term I use to describe the process of consuming wood by smouldering with the assistance of a draught whether induced naturally through the use of a smoke pipe or chimney setup or with the aid of a pumped air supply. There are several possibilities for supported smouldering; one of the simplest methods of achieving it is by generating a draught using a smoke pipe. I cover this effect in more detail later in the chapter called *the chimney effect*, see page 71. Other examples of this method of supported smouldering include the various types of smoke generators which use small air pumps to support the combustion process, providing an artificial draught.

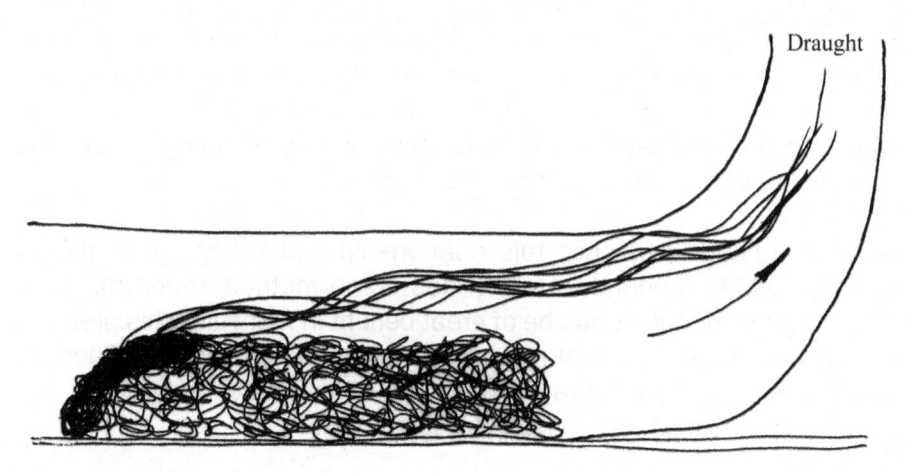

fig 7: supported smouldering utilising a draught

indirect heating

Indirect heating refers to the method of producing smoke by providing sufficient heat to decompose the wood, without the wood actually coming into contact with a direct flame or charcoal. This method is common in most stovetop food smokers where the wood dust or chips are held in a container away from the actual flame. It's the conducted heat which provides the necessary energy for the wood to decompose and produce smoke.

fig 8: indirect heating through a metal plate

This method of producing smoke is very reliable providing your heat supply is good and hot. One advantage of using this method is the production of PAHs (Polycyclic aromatic Hydrocarbons) is considered to be less than the equivalent direct smouldering method. It's worth noting that the indirect heating method doesn't rely on oxygen to combust the wood as the indirect heat is enough to decompose the wood. One food smoking product that could benefit from smoking specifically in an inert atmosphere is olive oil. Some high grade olive oils can benefit from not being exposed to the air for extended periods as this can significantly change the flavour characteristics of the oil. I have worked with one Spanish producer of olive oil on a setup to smoke in an oxygen-free environment using this method of indirect heating.

Enclosing wood chippings in a metal container which has perforations allowing the smoke to escape is a popular method of hot smoke generation. These devices are known as smoke caddies, smoke boxes or smoke pots. Essentially they all do the same thing, which is to create smoke through indirect heating of the wood chips or dust. Fill them half full with wood chips, close the lid and place the container on the hot coals. This method of pyrolysing wood chips produces excellent smoke whilst minimising flare-ups. There is also no need to soak the wood chips before using them to generate smoke and because the wood chips are contained inside the caddy or pot one is able to remove the device from the heat to stop further smoke being generated. Separating the coals from the wood prevents the likelihood of flare ups but it's worth noting that smoke is flammable in concentrations and if your barbeque is in flame from grilling fatty foods then it's likely these flames could ignite the smoke, so it's by no means a guarantee that you won't have a flare up but by using a caddy the chances will be greatly reduced.

direct heating

This method of producing smoke is by far the simplest and can be achieved by using either a sustained naked flame or the direct heat from a barbeque. By placing wood dust or chips directly onto the barbeque coals they are heated and start to decompose almost immediately producing copious amounts of smoke.

There is a danger using this method of a flare up where the smoke actually catches fire and this is more likely if you are using a gas barbeque or where you are cooking something that produces a lot of rendered fat on the barbeque which can drip onto the coals and cause flare ups. Make sure you have a water sprayer on hand to quench any flare ups if you adopt this approach. Dry wood shavings have a strong tendency to ignite. This is because they have a lot of air surrounding the individual shavings. To prevent this, or at least minimise the risk of it happening, lightly spray the shavings with clean water about an hour before use. This will allow the added moisture to be absorbed into the wood and prevent it from just catching fire.

fig 9: direct heating on charcoal

If this is your preferred method of producing smoke then a little tip for you is to soak a large quantity of your wood chips for a few hours, drain them well and then portion them into individual freezer bags and freeze them for future barbeques. You can have access to wood chips any time of the year without having to wait for the wood to soak first and they can be used straight from the freezer.

generating smoke

There are a number of different methods used to burn wood to produce smoke. What follow covers some of the more popular methods for generating smoke from dust chips and chunks and will provide an insight into some of the tricks of the trade. Due to all the variables in the combustion process it is advisable to adopt a flexible approach to generating smoke and to view failure as a sign that you are one step closer to mastering the art.

the cold smoke generator

This cold smoke generator is a simple maze-type burn tray which incorporates a spiral maze pattern. This spiral pattern forces the burn to follow the spiral path. The ProQ is one type of cold smoke generator that performs at its best when used with fine wood dust. This is a particularly elegant smoke generator for small applications like a cardboard smoker or small cabinet. The ProQ smoke generator is made from stainless steel mesh with a stainless steel wire frame. The stainless steel mesh used on this generator is particularly fine. This is important for two reasons. Firstly, metal tends to draw heat away from the combustion process and this could lead to combustion ceasing, making the generator unreliable. Secondly, the fine mesh allows air to pass through it into the wood dust, assisting and supporting the combustion process. There are similar arrangements to the maze type smoke generator. One particular design is a rectangular out-and-return smoke generator made and marketed by smokedust.co.uk which has the capability to produce smoke for approximately twelve hours.

fig 10: ProQ smoke generator

Both these natural-smouldering, burn-tray smoke generators have as part of their design a finite burn width. This makes them reliable in terms of the burn duration and the amount of heat they produce. This is particularly important when cold smoking as the temperature should be kept as low as possible.

fig 11: smoke dust large burn tray

The ProQ generator is a cold smoke generator and it's very good at what it does. The width of the maze pattern has the effect of restricting the size of the burn front which in turn limits the amount of heat that can be generated from the combustion process and it's this which makes is perfect for small scale cold smoking. The small burn front is the key to the effectiveness of the generator in restricting the size of burn and thus slowing the combustion process to the point where this smoke generator can sustain a burn from six to ten hours.

The fine dust which this generator uses has to be dry or it will have a tendency to self-extinguish. To overcome this problem, the wood dust needs to be dry enough to sustain combustion. To achieve this it's worth just placing the generator (with the wood already loaded) into a pre-heated oven for about ten minutes. This should be sufficient time to drive off any unwanted moisture and make the combustion more reliable.

fig 12: ProQ smoke generator loaded with wood dust

the Venturi principle smoke generator

This smoke generator relies on the effect known as the Venturi effect. The Venturi effect relates to fluids but can be equally applied to gases like air and smoke. Simply put, when a gas is passed through a restriction its velocity increases as it passes through the restriction and as it does so its pressure drops due to the principles of conservation of energy. Fig 13 shows this effect and how it can be used inside a smoke generator to induce an airflow, which in turn can be used to support combustion.

This effect is so reliable when set up correctly in a smoke generator it is possible to get small chunks and wood chips to smoulder when otherwise, if left to their own devices, they would normally self-extinguish. This can be very useful as it's not always possible to get hold of fine wood dust unless you purchase it directly, whereas it's well within the scope of the home smoker to make wood chips using a garden chipper.

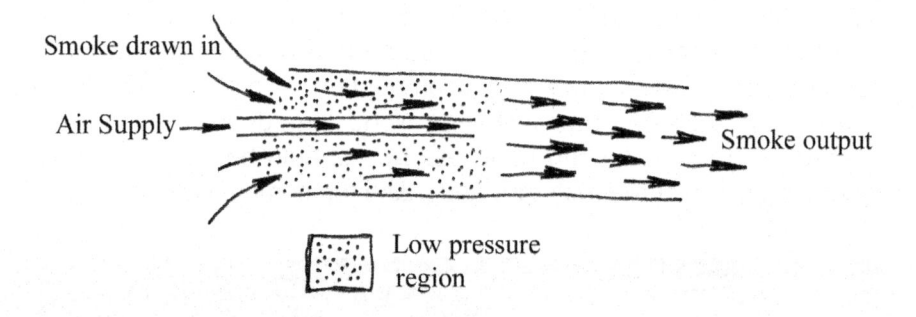

fig 13: the Venturi effect simplified

To utilise this effect in generating smoke is relatively easy. There are several incarnations of Venturi smoke generators on the market but the one common factor amongst them is the need for an air pump to provide the supply of air. Under normal circumstances it is only necessary to provide a very small amount of air and therefore a small pump is all that is needed. Using a small fish tank air pump is sufficient for this purpose.

These are usually run from the mains electricity supply and as food smoking is an outdoor pursuit one must exercise due caution when using electrical equipment operating from the mains supply outdoors.

Smoke generators using the Venturi principle have grown in popularity over the past few years and there is now a wide variety available on the market for those wishing to spend lots of money. If you would prefer to have a go at constructing one yourself I have included a few instructions on how do so.

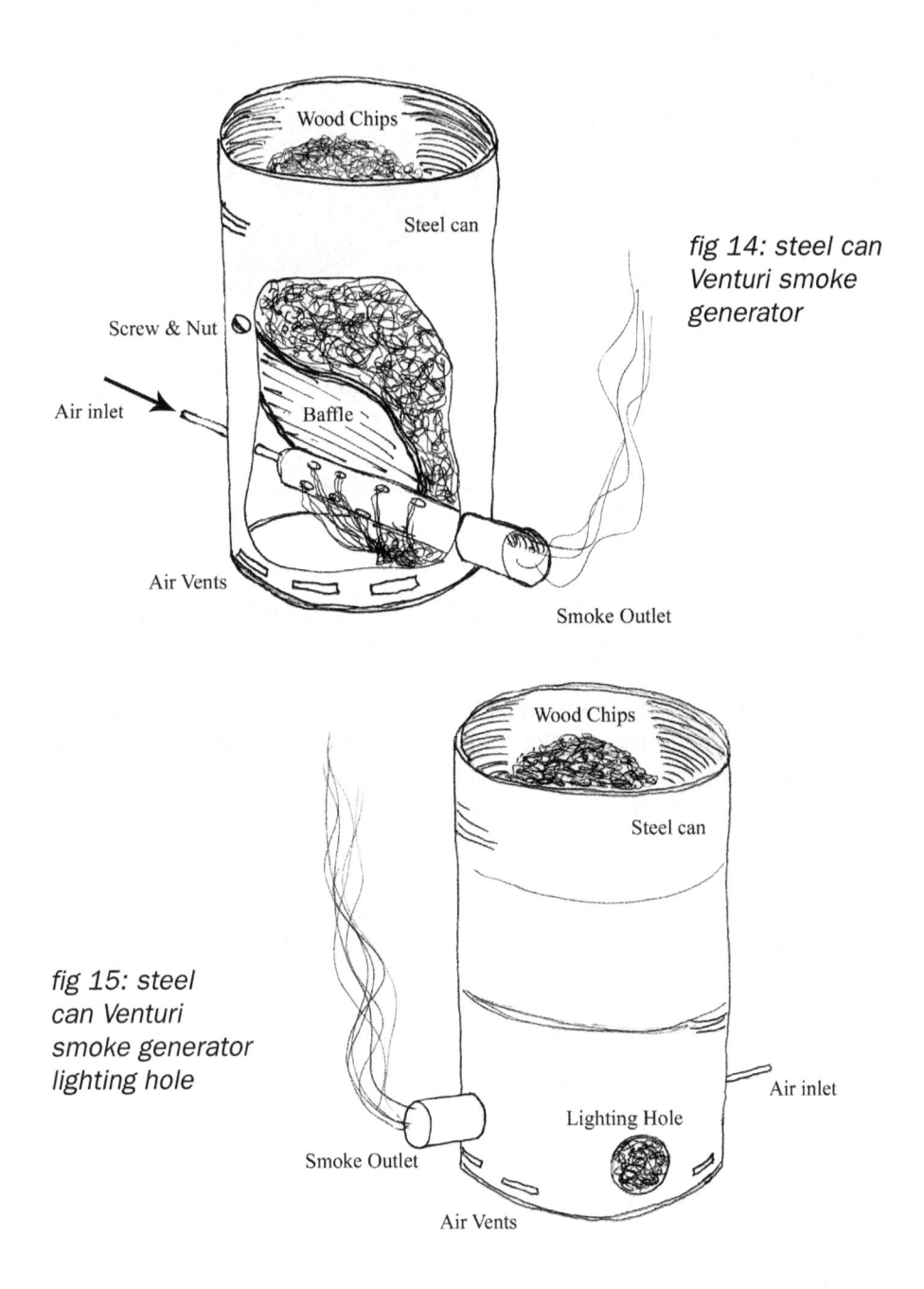

fig 14: steel can Venturi smoke generator

fig 15: steel can Venturi smoke generator lighting hole

This kind of smoke generator is simple and cost effective to make. Firstly, select a suitable steel can. An old baked bean or tomato can will do. Make sure before use that you burn off all the internal protective lacquer coating on the inside, which is there to protect the product and stop the

LILI *food smoking* 67

product reacting with the metal coating. The coating will impart a nasty flavour when burnt if it isn't removed so this step is really important. Keep hold of the lid as this will be used as a baffle. The baffle stops the smoke tube from becoming clogged with wood dust, allowing it to remain clear so the air flows through the Venturi tube.

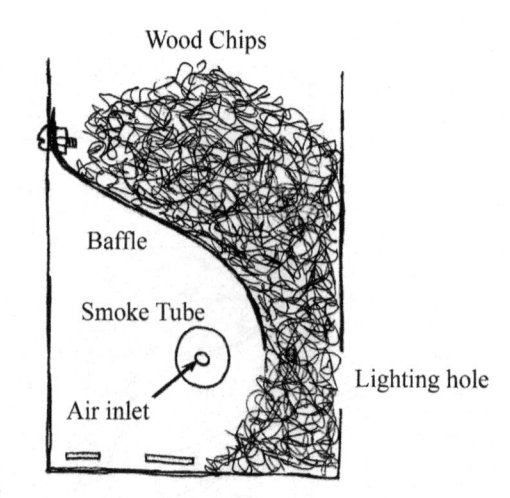

fig 16: steel can Venturi smoke generator side view

Fig 17 shows a cross section of the can showing the baffle and how it works to keep the wood chips away from the smoke tube.

The smoke tube can be made from 22mm diameter copper tube. The air inlet tube sits inside the smoke tube and can be made from small bore steel or stainless steel tube. 4 or 5mm diameter tubing should be fine for this purpose. Some model stores sell this size tubing. The smoke pipe should have a series of holes drilled approximately half way along its length to allow smoke to enter. The air inlet tube sits inside the smoke tube. The end of the air inlet tube should be inserted past the holes drilled in the side of the smoke tube as shown in fig 17.

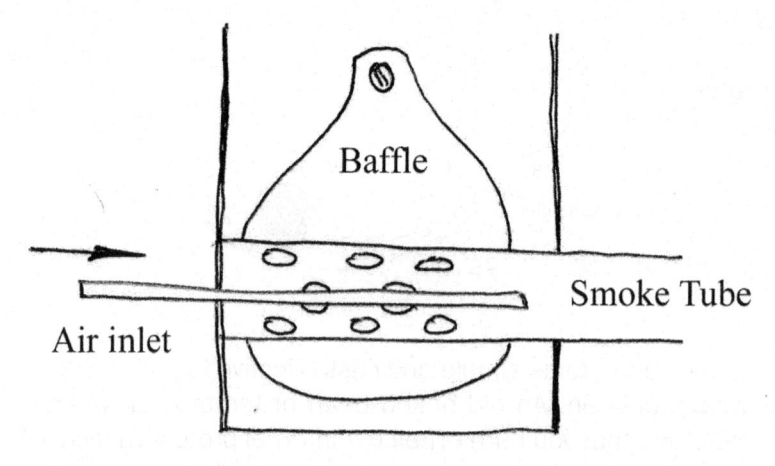

fig 17: steel can Venturi smoke generator cross section

68 food smoking L I L I

There are variations on this bean can smoke generator which can be seen in fig 14-15

Not all smoke generators have to be that complicated. The idea that you can just light a smoke generator and forget about it is a lovely thought – especially when you consider smoking food takes time and having to keep tending it can be a little tedious. Using wood dust may well be the best way to ensure reliable smouldering but this may not always be available to the home food smoker. If you have access to good quality shavings you may need to adopt another approach to sustain a reliable smoulder.

foil package smoke generator

There is a very simple way to produce smoke if you haven't got the time or energy to construct or purchase one of the smoke generators I've already mentioned. One of the simplest methods of creating smoke is to create a foil package of wood chips or dust with a series of holes pierced in the top.

Place this on a barbeque and hey presto – smoke. This method is pretty reliable and controllable as it allows you to remove the package from the coals with a pair of tongs as a means of regulating the smoke it produces. I have used this method on several occasions in the past and I'm often asked if the aluminium reacts with the heat to produce undesirable residue or deposits on the food. There is no direct evidence to suggest this is the case. Aluminium melts at 660°C and charcoal temperatures can exceed this figure depending on the availability of oxygen. On average a barbeque has a charcoal temperature of around 550°C to 700°C so there is a very slight chance the foil will melt but this is only likely in extreme circumstances. Placing the package off to a cooler part of the barbeque will do the trick as wood will start to decompose into smoke at much lower temperatures, typically in the range of 200°C and 300°C which is way before the foil will begin to melt. It is likely that the foil will oxidise while in contact with the charcoal and when this happens the aluminium oxide formed will provide further protection as this won't degrade further until it is subjected to temperatures in excess of 2000°C.

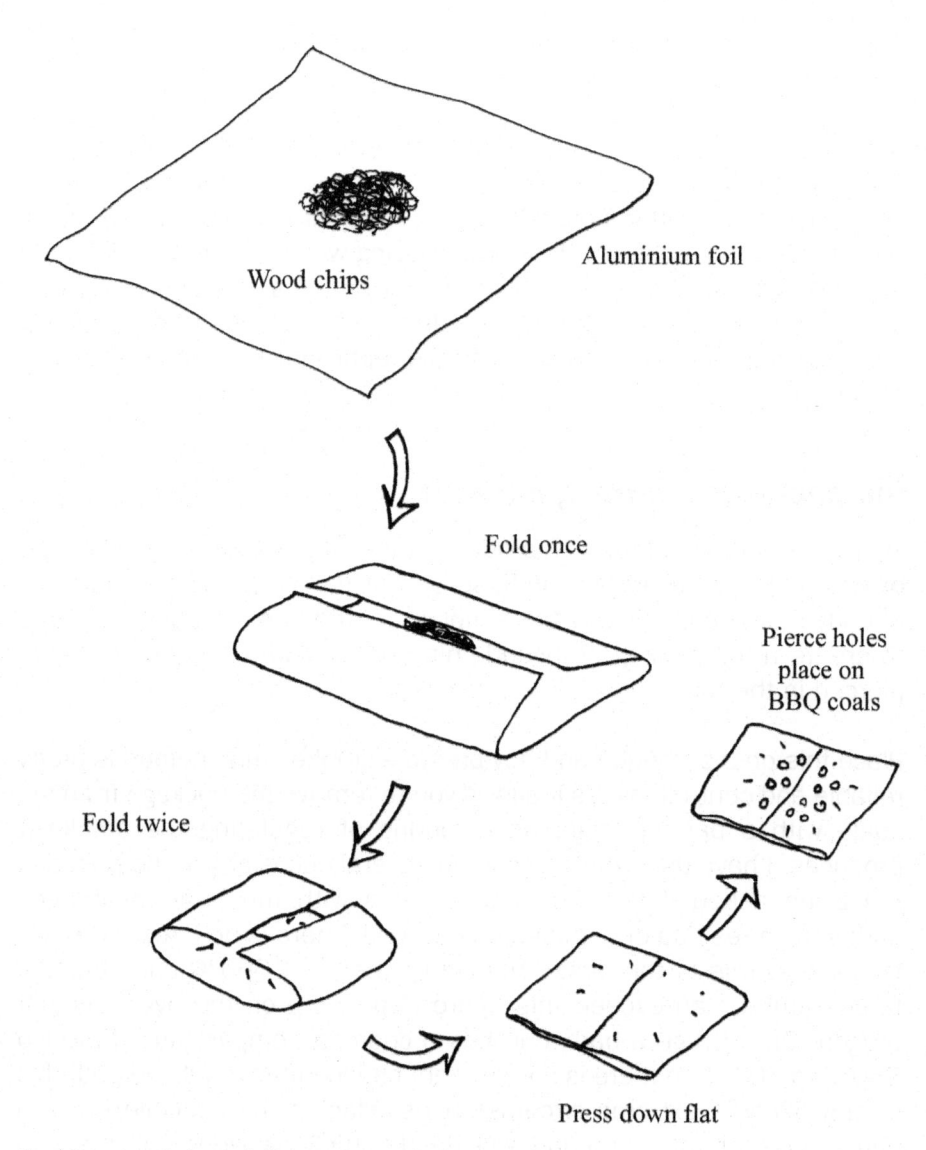

fig 18: aluminium foil smoke generator

the chimney effect

Enjoying the warming glow from a real fire can stir up primeval feelings of safety and security. There's something about a real fire that can lift the spirit and warm the heart on a cold night. The heat fire gives us is certainly high up on the list of priorities for survival along with food and drink but we often forget about the ingenious and often innovative steps we have taken to bring fire into our homes. In days gone by the only way we heated our dwellings was to bring the fire indoors and utilise its warmth at the same time as using that same ingenuity to eject the gases that were not so good for us. Not the Roman hypocaust for most of us, no, that was the preserve of the rich. Open fires in the middle of the room were more common and later hearths and chimneys to contain the fire and eject the products of combustion. A basic chimney operates on the very simple principle of gas buoyancy. We see the very same principle in operation in a simple smoker set up using a remote smoke pipe as seen in fig 19.

The chimney effect, draw or draught as it is sometimes referred to in a chimney, is an integral part of food smoking if you are using a remote smoke generator or fire pit where you are looking to draw smoke from a remote source into the smoker.

buoyancy

The idea that hot gases rise can be explained using the hot air analogy: when a given volume of air is heated it expands. This is one of the basic gas laws called Charles' law, which states that for a constant pressure, a given volume of gas will increase its volume in direct proportion to its temperature. As it does this it will by definition become less dense than the surrounding gas that hasn't been heated and will, as a result of this relative difference in density, have a tendency to rise. Wrap this up in a long vertical tube and you have the basic principle of how a chimney works. And if you are using a smoke pipe to deliver smoke from a heat source to a smoking cabinet you are essentially using the same buoyancy mechanism to get the smoke into the smoker as a chimney uses to eject smoke from a fire place and into the flue.

Damper partially open

Air flow

Smoke Pipe

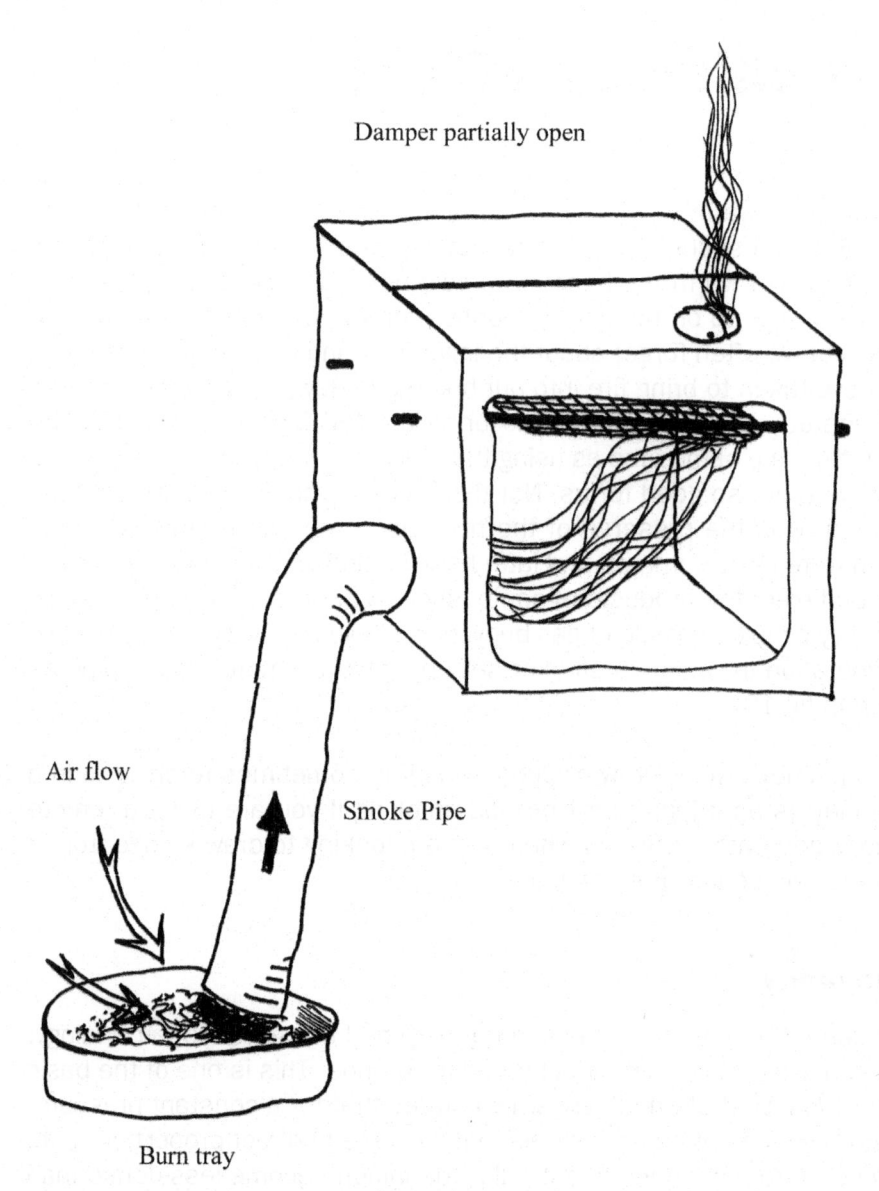

Burn tray

fig 19: an example of a smoker using a remote smoke pipe

Controlling gas flow within the chimney can present a few challenges especially when you consider the strength of draught/draw that can be generated from a long chimney full of buoyant warm smoke and gas. Under these conditions the flow of smoke and gases up the chimney or smoke pipe can have the effect of drawing more air into the area where the smoke is being generated. Whilst this is desirable in moderation, one can end up with a runaway effect of more air being force fed to the area of combustion producing faster combustion which can ultimately lead to flames, heat and little or no smoke, and in turn produce more heat and a greater draught/draw from the chimney causing even more vigorous combustion; not a good position to be in as I think you'd agree.

damper

One way of controlling the draught/draw is to use what is known as a damper. This is a simple device which does nothing more than to restrict the airflow in the system.

Damper position

Airflow

Temperature

Smoke production

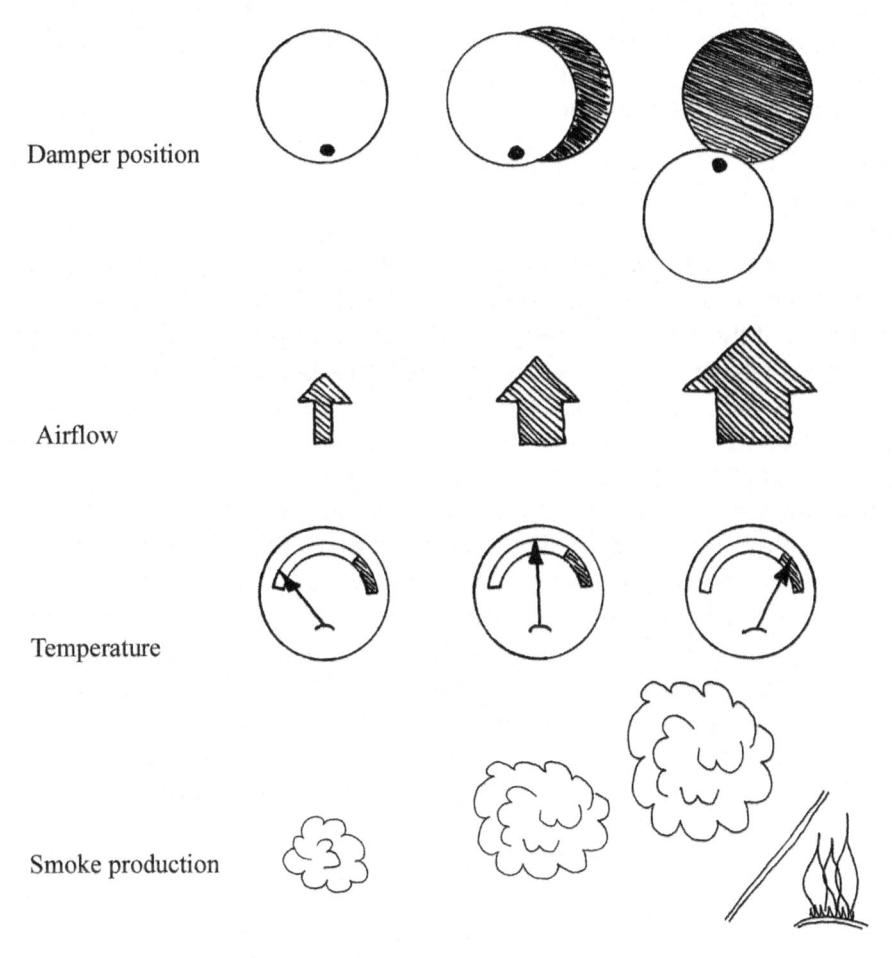

fig 20: the relationship between damper setting, heat and smoke production

The damper can either be at the end of the system restricting the smoke leaving the system or it can be at the beginning of the system restricting the air entering the system. Where the damper is at the end of the system, the damper will only work properly if the other parts of the system between the damper and the fire box are sealed. Most food smokers, if fitted with a damper have it fitted at the end of the system restricting the smoke leaving the smoker. There are a few smokers where the air supply to the smoke generator is the only mechanism to control the rate of combustion in the system and this is completely acceptable, and in many ways preferable to the other methods of control, as restricting the amount of oxygen reaching the combustion does not rely on the integrity of the pipework or smoking cabinet to limit the potential for unrestricted airflow to the area of combustion. Fig 20 shows a pictorial representation of the relationship between the damper, smoke production and heat production.

heat

The chimney effect or draught/draw, as described previously, is primarily driven by heat and the effect heat has on a given mass of air by giving it buoyancy. If there is insufficient heat in the system to ensure the smoke continues into the smoker and out through the damper, the draught/draw effect can come to a standstill and smoke will plateau in either the pipe or the smoker. The technical word for this is stratification and is only really relevant in large or tall smokers or very long smoke pipes where one is relying totally on natural ventilation and there are no mechanical means to assist flow. Stratification occurs when the temperature of the rising smoke in the pipe or smoker naturally loses its heat and cools to the same temperature as the surrounding air in the pipe or smoker. When this happens the difference in temperature between the surrounding atmosphere and the smoke is zero and as a result of that lack of difference, the smoke effectively loses its buoyancy and instead of rising as it did previously it begins to build up at one level and spread out to form a strata or horizontal layer, hence the name stratification.

It's unlikely you will encounter this type of issue using a small smoker or relatively short smoke pipe. There is a point to consider here, especially if you are cold smoking, that there is a need to lose as much of the heat in the smoke as is possible while maintaining a small amount of residual heat to ensure buoyancy is maintained and the smoke still draws naturally into the smoker. This heat balancing act is easy enough to manage by adopting a few neat tricks and of course by maintaining a keen eye on what you are doing.

If using a smoke pipe to supply your smoking cabinet there are a number of different methods you can adopt to manage the heat that is produced along with the smoke to ensure not too much of it gets into the smoking cabinet affecting the food. An old tried and tested method for this kind of smoker is to bury the smoke pipe so it completely covered by earth. Obviously one will have to consider the design and site layout before constructing a smoker using this method. By doing this, any heat from the smoke can be readily absorbed through the smoke pipe and into the ground before having a chance of being transmitted into the smoking cabinet.

Provided the smoke pipe is entirely in contact with the surrounding earth and providing the smoke pipe is made from a material which readily conducts heat, any unwanted additional heat will pass directly into the surrounding earth leaving the remaining smoke considerably cooler than when it was produced. One consideration here is the simple fact that smoke in itself is a condensate and will also have a tendency to condense out onto the inside of the smoke pipe as it travels along into the smoking cabinet. This effect will be relatively small and to avoid a build-up of residue in the pipe a gentle fall or slope should be designed into the smoke pipe to allow this smoke condensate or any other residue to gently run back towards the fire box. There may be occasions where the surrounding earth is very dry and doesn't readily assist in acting as a heat sink for the smoke pipe. If this is the case it is advisable to soak the ground above the smoke pipe. Water is an extremely effective heat sink and has an enormous capability for absorbing heat. To give you an idea of its effectiveness, it takes 4,187 Joules of energy to raise the temperature of 1kg of water by 1°C. By adding water to the ground the smoke pipe runs in you are effectively increasing the ability the ground has to absorb heat and do the job you want it to.

Some smokers are designed to be a little more portable than the underground smoke pipe design and incorporate an above ground smoke pipe. This can be made from any material providing it is not readily combustible or does not react adversely with the smoke. Using a material that readily conducts heat and is flexible or extendable can be a real benefit if adjustments are needed to control the heat entering the smoker.

Greater area for heat to radiate through the smoke pipe will deliver cooler smoke into the smoker

Long Smoke pipe

Damper

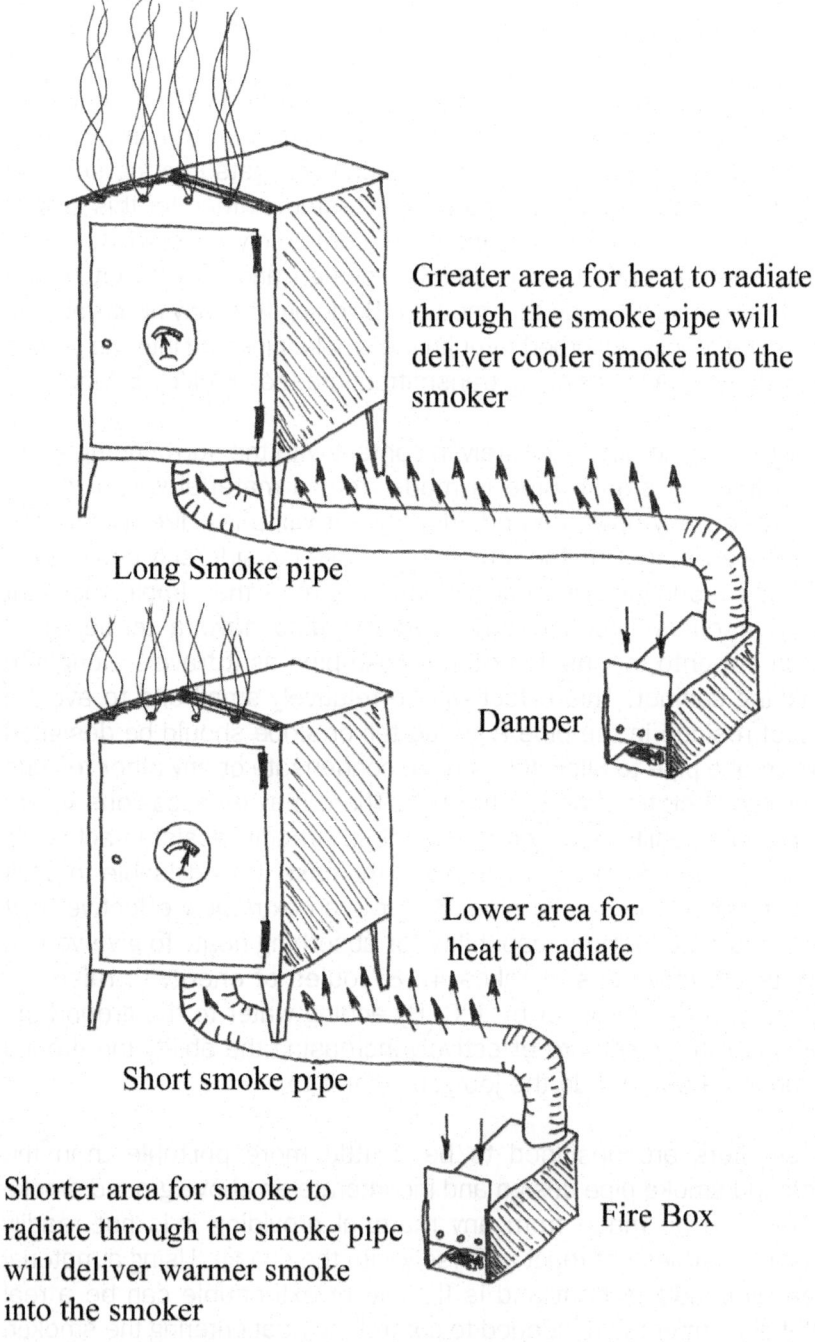

Lower area for heat to radiate

Short smoke pipe

Shorter area for smoke to radiate through the smoke pipe will deliver warmer smoke into the smoker

Fire Box

fig 21: regulating the heat by extending the smoke pipe

When using a remote smoke source the design of the smoker is critical when it comes to controlling the heat entering the smoker. Another effective method for controlling or regulating the heat without having to alter the combustion process is to introduce horizontal spacing between the smoke source and the smoker. This will effectively force the smoke to travel sideways along the smoke pipe allowing a portion of the heat to be lost to the pipe before it gets to the smoker as in fig 21.

By adjusting this distance one can regulate or control the amount of heat lost to the pipe thus controlling the heat that eventually gets into the smoker. I have used this method on a number of occasions and it works well. I use a flexible metal ducting which allows these length adjustments quite easily with little fuss.

I have even modified the horizontal pipe method when the heat getting to the smoker is excessive by the addition of a wet cloth draped over the top of the pipe to assist in absorbing some of the heat. Remember earlier when I mentioned the wet earth on the underground pipe and how this absorbed heat, well the same method works with the above ground smoke pipe by using towels soaked in water. The key is to separate the heat from the smoke the best way you can.

the smoke spreader

The smoke spreader is used inside the smoker to do exactly what it suggests, spread smoke! When not influenced by air currents, smoke has a natural tendency to rise in a vertical column. Ordinarily, smoke rising inside a smoker is a desirable thing. Most smokers employ vertical food racks which are designed to allow smoke to pass up through them. Where smoke is introduced into the smoker by a remote smoke pipe, the cross-sectional area of that pipe will determine the cross-sectional area of the smoke as it enters the smoker, especially if the smoke pipe enters in the centre of the base. It's quite possible for a narrow column of smoke to form above the smoke pipe. In larger smokers, if the smoke is not spread out evenly across the entire cross-sectional area of the smoking cabinet there is a likelihood that the smoke could miss food that is not directly in its path as it rises through and out through the damper. This is not so much of an issue for food at the top of the smoker as the smoke will have a tendency to spread out a little across the whole cross-sectional area of the smoker as it rises. The main concern is for any food being smoked in the lower parts of the smoker. Without the smoke spreader this area of the smoker would be missed completely rendering it almost ineffective. Any food in this area won't benefit from the smoke.

To guard against parts of the smoker not getting any smoke, the smoke spreader is designed to allow the smoke to spread out over the entire cross-sectional area of the smoker before allowing it to pass through holes into the smoking cabinet and up through the food racks, evenly smoking the food.

By introducing a barrier in the area between where the smoke enters the smoker and the food racks, the smoker can be made to operate more efficiently, utilising more rack space in parts of the smoker that wouldn't normally receive as much smoke as the upper reaches of the smoke cabinet if it weren't for the smoke spreader.

In terms of design, when constructing the smoke spreader it's sensible to make sufficient holes across the whole cross-sectional area to allow the entire body of smoke to rise through into the smoking compartment.

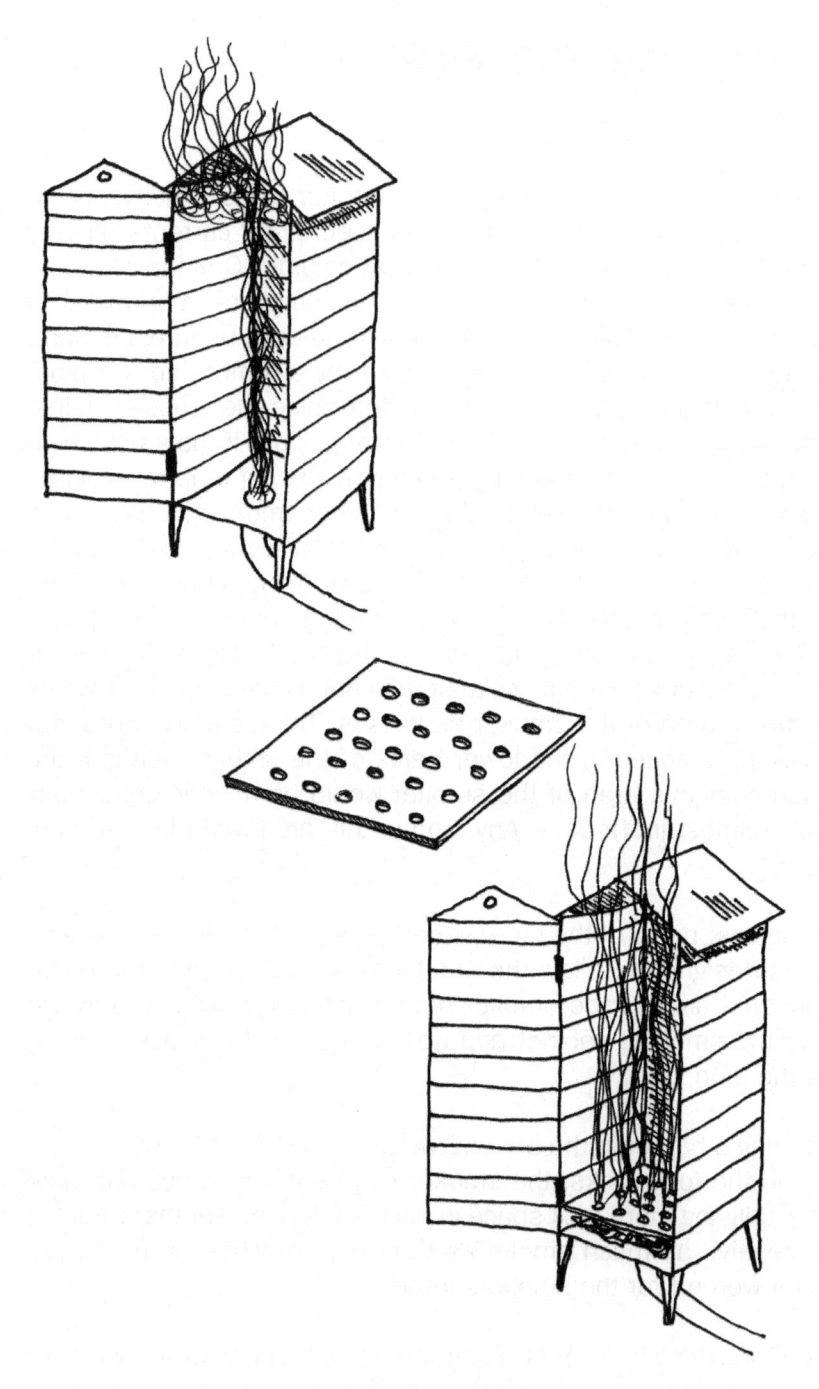

fig 22: the effect of the smoke spreader

In order to achieve this, one should aim to balance the total area of the holes in the smoke spreader to that of the cross-sectional area of the smoke pipe. In order to achieve a balance, the following table, fig 23, sets out the optimum number and size of holes required in the smoke spreader for a given diameter of smoke pipe.

The matrix shows the minimum number of holes required for a smoke spreader

Smoke pipe diameter (mm)

Sq. mm	50	60	70	80	90	100	120	130	140	150
	1964	2828	3849	5027	6363	7855	11311	13275	15396	17674
10mm	79	25	36	49	64	81	100	144	169	196	225
15mm	177	11	16	22	28	36	44	64	75	87	100
20mm	314	6	9	12	16	20	25	36	42	49	56
25mm	491	4	6	8	10	13	16	23	27	31	36

optimum number of holes required for a smoke spreader

Smoke pipe diameter (mm)

Sq. mm	50	60	70	80	90	100	120	130	140	150
	1964	2828	3849	5027	6363	7855	11311	13275	15396	17674
10mm	79	38	54	74	96	122	150	216	254	294	338
15mm	177	17	24	33	43	54	67	96	113	131	150
20mm	314	9	14	18	24	30	38	54	63	74	84
25mm	491	6	9	12	15	19	24	35	41	47	54

fig 23: smoke spreader design

cardboard food smoker

WARNING
Cardboard is combustible and this smoker should always be used responsibly by ensuring the smoke source is separated from contact with the surfaces of the smoker. Always place the smoke generator on a metal tray and never use naked flames in or near this smoker.

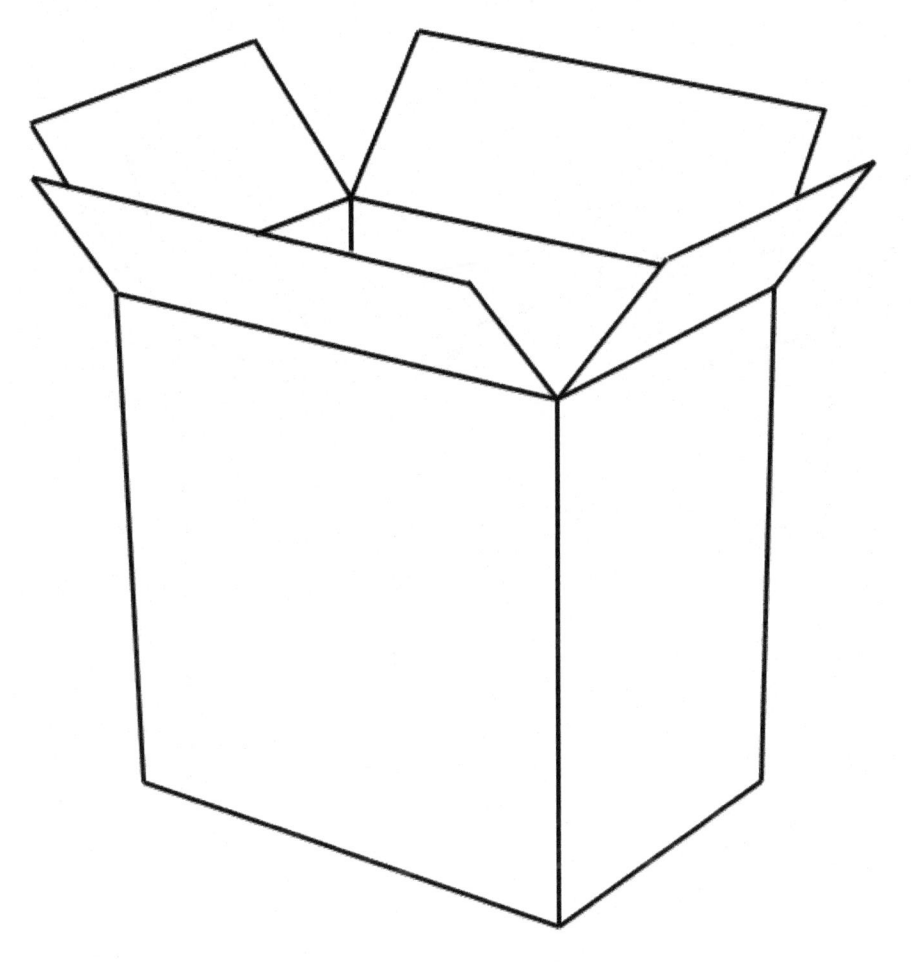

fig 24: cardboard box

This device is designed for cold smoking only using the ProQ smoke generator or a remote cold smoke source. You have been warned.

getting started

Start your smoker with a good quality cardboard box. It's not too important that it has a base but ensure the lid can close completely. To complete this project you will need the following items: 2 standard wire cake racks (375mm X 260mm), 2.5 metres of 9mm wooden dowel, duct tape, a craft knife, a pin or small nail, pair of scissors and a tape measure. The racks will rest on the dowel to form shelves for the food.

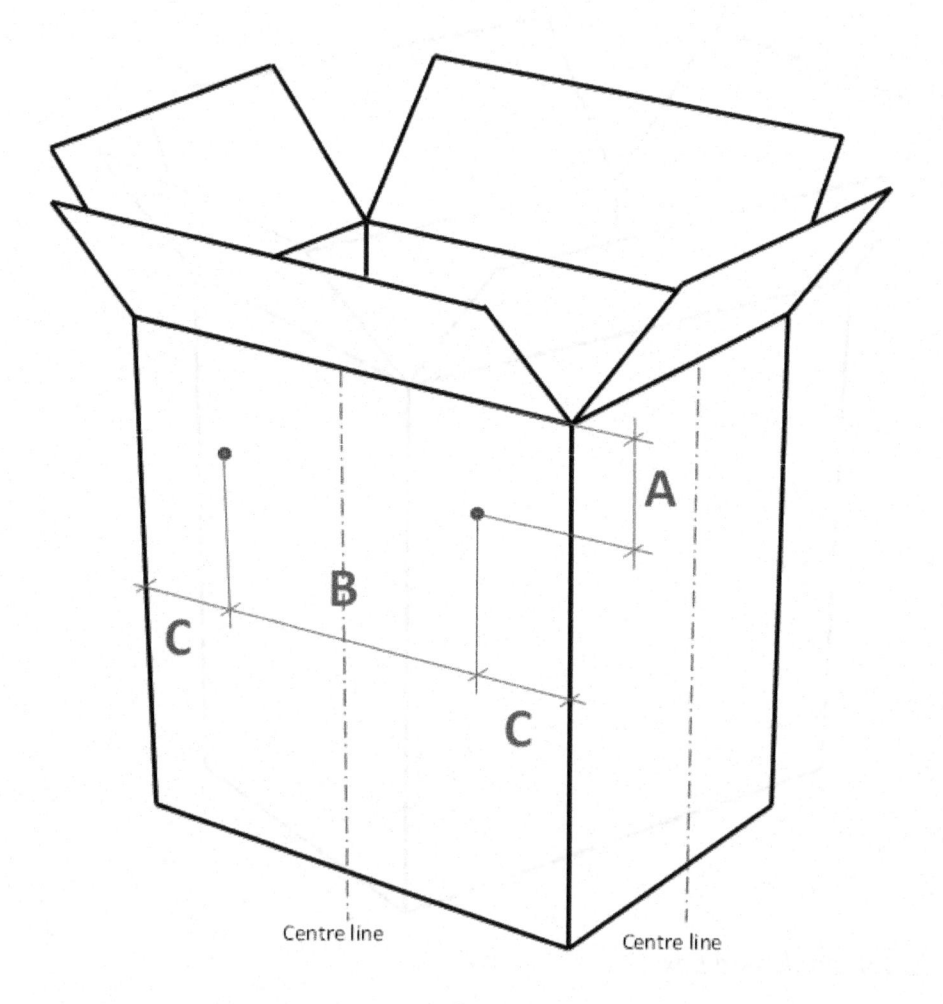

fig 25: cardboard box layout for marking holes

84 food smoking **LILI**

In fig 26 dimensions for setting out the holes for the support dowels are as follows:

    A = 100 mm; to install a lower smoking rack make a second set of dowel holes 200mm from the top of the box.
    B = 320 mm. This is the width between the wooden dowels that the food racks will eventually rest on.
    C = the exact size in mm depends on the size of your cardboard box.

A good tip to help you centre the racks is to find the centre line of the box and then measure 'B', divide that by 2 = 160mm. Measure 160mm either side of the centre line and make your marks for the wooden dowels.

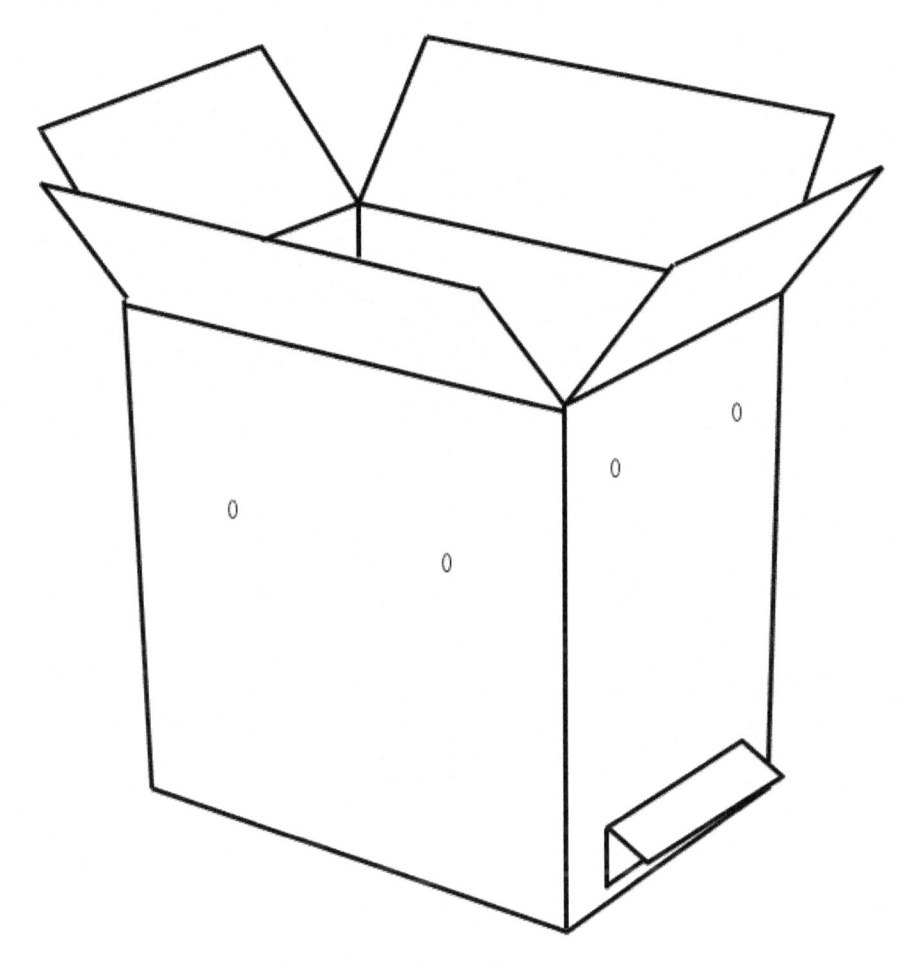

fig 26: cardboard box with access flap

After making the holes in the side of the box, reinforce them with a small strip of duct tape. This principle can be applied to all the edges of your smoker to increase rigidity and add a little structure to the cardboard smoker. It will last longer that way.

An access flap needs to be created so you can insert, inspect and get at your smoke generator. 250mm wide by around 100mm high as close to the base of the box as possible. Ensure it's big enough to remove the smoke generator by hand. This flap can be reinforced with duct tape to add rigidity in the same way as the sides and edges.

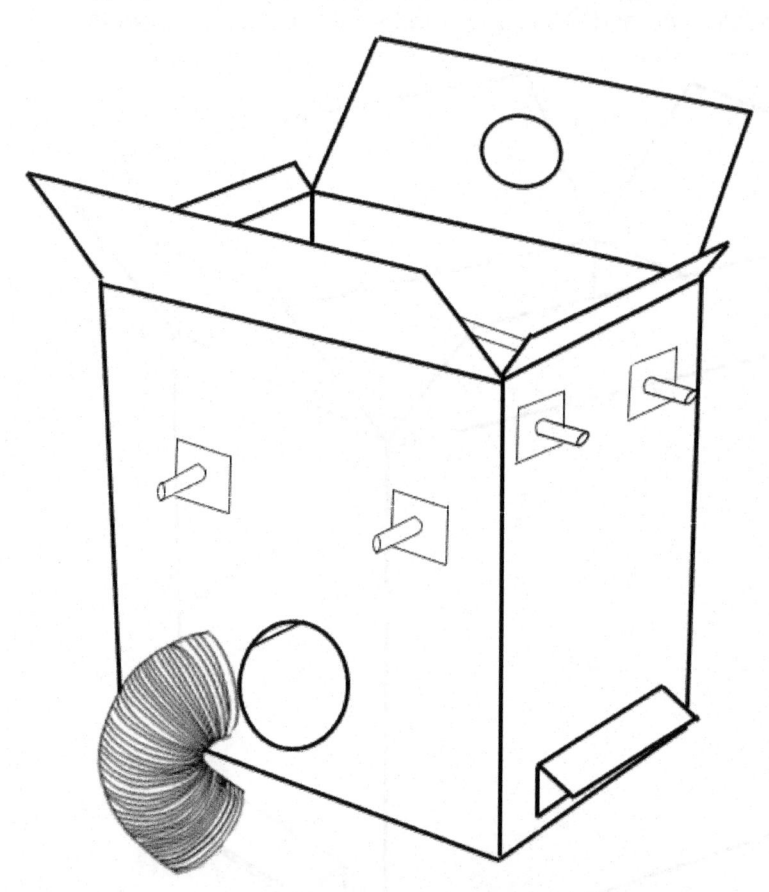

fig 27: cardboard box smoker with dowels in place

Holes will need to be made on the opposite face of the cardboard box to those marked in the diagram. These are so the supporting dowels can pass all the way through the box remaining level. Make these at the same height as the first set of holes so the food racks can sit as level as possible on the wooden dowels. Only two of the holes on each side are shown in fig 26. The dowels pass all the way through the box. You will need to trim down a couple of the box flaps and a good tip is to use the discarded cardboard as a height gauge template for marking the holes on the opposite side of the box.

Insert the hard wood dowels through the box. These dowels will act as a rest for the wire racks you'll place your food on when you get the smoker to work. It's important that they are level and parallel so your food won't roll off to one side and the rack will remain evenly supported.

To generate smoke remotely from the smoker, cut a 100mm hole in the side and connect to your smoke source with some suitable non-combustible ducting. The cut out can be used as a damper on the lid of the smoker. Flexible aluminium ducting is suitable for this purpose and can be purchased from most reputable DIY stores.

If using the remote smoke source it may be necessary to use a damper to control the combustion process. Cut an approximately 75mm diameter hole. This will act as a damper. Use the 100mm cut out from the hole cut for the smoke pipe as the cover for the damper and use a small paper staple or nail to make a hinge.

Fig 27 shows that the cardboard box has had a pair of its flaps cut down. It's important to choose the set of flaps that don't meet in the middle or you will be left with a cardboard box that doesn't close fully. Cut down these flaps so they are only about 50mm in length. The reason for trimming these flaps is to ensure they don't droop down inside the box and touch the food.

using the cardboard smoker

This is a wonderful little smoker that can transform good food into great food with minimal expense. It may seem a little counter intuitive to use what is essentially a combustible container and then introduce the products of combustion into it blindly hoping things will turn out OK. Of course to utilise a cardboard box for smoking food without first taking the necessary precautions to ensure it was safe to use would be a pretty foolish thing to do. So, the first thing that should be understood is that a cardboard box can only be used for cold smoking. Due to the restrictions in the level of heat used for cold smoking (below 30°C) the cardboard smoker is ideal and actually has some clear benefits over a traditional metal cold smoker which I will mention later. Whenever I demonstrate the use of the cardboard smoker I always emphasise the need to make safety the first priority not only in terms of fire but food safety too. I would always recommend using a new cardboard box or at the very least one which is clean and dry. Introducing smoke into the cardboard smoker can be done in two ways, either by introducing a smoke generator into the body of the cardboard smoker or by supplying the smoke into the cardboard smoker through a remote pipe connected to the smoke source.

Introducing a smoke generator into the body of the cardboard smoker is only possible if using a device like the ProQ smoke generator which is an extremely safe device for this kind of application. The ProQ smoke generator produces only miniscule amounts of heat which is only ever going to produce a gentle smoulder. It's almost unheard of for this kind of smoke generator to initiate flaming combustion which is mainly due to the nature and fine composition of the wood dust used it. This makes this smoke generator ideal for use inside the cardboard smoker. To use the ProQ smoke generator safely inside the cardboard smoker it will need to sit firmly on a metal tray or baking dish. This is a precaution against any burning embers dropping beneath the generator and setting fire to the cardboard. The ProQ generator produces a gentle smoke for anywhere between six to ten hours so is ideal for use in this application.

Introducing smoke from a remote source is for many the safest approach, providing the source of the smoke is not generating too much heat to cause problems inside the cardboard smoker, which I will come onto in a moment. Transferring the smoke from its source to the smoker can be achieved by using a smoke pipe or other non-combustible means. I have used flexible metal ducting similar to that used for cooker hoods which has proved very effective. Getting the smoke to flow into the smoker should be quite a simple affair and the best method for achieving this is to use the natural buoyancy of warm smoke. Warm smoke or smoke that is warmer than the ambient outside air temperature has a tendency to rise. By utilising this simple principle one can construct an arrangement where the cardboard smoker is positioned at a higher level than the smoke source allowing the smoke to rise into the smoker under its own steam.

If the smoke entering the flexible pipe is too warm for cold smoking and there is a need to cool it down before it enters the smoker; this can be achieved by one of two methods. Either by extending the flexible metal pipe so the smoke has to travel further along its length, dissipating heat as it travels along into the smoker, or by draping the metal pipe with damp cloths or sheets of wetted newspaper so they absorb the heat energy from the smoke before it gets to the smoker. Because metal ducting conducts heat very efficiently, the heat from the smoke is naturally drawn away as it comes into contact with the inner surface of the pipe and is dissipated into the atmosphere. The heat from the smoke is absorbed through raising the temperature of the damp cloth or sheets of wetted newspaper lying on the pipe. I have found this method of control a little haphazard as it takes active monitoring which at times can be a little tiresome especially when you're smoking food for twelve hours.

the damper

The damper on the lid of the cardboard smoker is there to control the flow of smoke into the smoking compartment when using a remote smoke source that is being fed from a smoke pipe. By adjusting the damper one can regulate the amount of air that can leave the smoker and thus regulate the amount of smoke that can enter the smoker. By default, if you trace this back to the source of the smoke, the damper has a direct influence on the amount of air available for the combustion process. This an important point to remember because if the damper is left open while a remote smoke source is connected, the draught/draw that is set up between the cardboard smoker and the smoke source can run away with itself causing too much heat and ultimately flaming combustion. For a cardboard smoker this is a bad thing as the last thing one wants is a roaring chimney feeding into the bottom of one's smoker, especially when it's made from cardboard. This would not only ruin your day but more than likely your food too. For this reason the damper is an important piece of equipment even on a cardboard smoker.

When the cardboard smoker is being used with the ProQ smoke generator it is normal to leave the damper slightly open to allow smoke and moisture to escape during cold smoking. The small access flap cut into the side of the cardboard smoker is all that is needed to supply oxygen to maintain combustion and it only needs to be left slightly ajar to be effective.

The first thing to do when using the cardboard smoker is to ensure the cardboard box is clean and in good shape. Make sure the box is placed outside in the open air. I've been using the same cardboard smoker for about two years and unless I can guarantee the weather is going to be as advertised I always ensure the gazebo is up to protect it from rain. I also have a nice little cardboard box for smoking small amounts of cheese and I protect this year round with an old golfing umbrella when the weather threatens.

loading the smoker

To load the smoker, insert the dowels into the holes that have been made for the lower food rack. Once you have placed the first food racks on the supporting dowels and put your prepared food on them, the upper level dowels can be inserted for the final food racks and food. The smoker is now ready for closing up. It is advisable to use duct tape on all the edges of the lid to ensure a good seal. Ensure the damper is slightly open. You're now ready to introduce the smoke generator to the smoker. Simply light it and once you're satisfied it's going, pop it on a metal tray or baking dish and insert the smoke generator on the tray through the access flap in the side of the smoker. If you are using a remote smoke source, ensure there's a good seal for the smoke pipe and that the smoke temperature is correct. Check for the first ten or so minutes to make sure the smoke comes out through the damper and once you're satisfied it is working you can visit it every couple of hours to see how it's progressing.

Although I have not shown it in the previous diagrams I advise the use of a temperature probe when the smoker is in use. The temperature probe is there to give some reassurance that the temperature remains within safe limits below the critical temperature of 30°C. To use a temperature probe effectively it will need to be positioned through the side of the smoker at the same level as the highest food rack. This can be achieved simply by poking a hole through the cardboard and inserting the probe. It's possible to securely attach the temperature probe to the side of the smoker with self-adhesive hook and eye tape.

It's advisable to use the cardboard smoker away from direct sunlight as cardboard is really good at absorbing solar radiation. Using the cardboard smoker in direct sunlight can add around 20°C to the ambient temperature and make cold smoking almost impossible. However in shade and using the ProQ smoke generator I can cold smoke food in the low 20s all day long. If the weather is just too hot to cold smoke during the day I wait until nightfall and take advantage of the cooler temperatures.

advantages of using the cardboard smoker

Using the cardboard smoker with the ProQ smoke generator couldn't be simpler. Fire and forget is the order of the day. It really is a joy to use. Using cardboard has some distinct advantages over traditional smokers as I mentioned briefly earlier. With the growing interest in gourmet foods and specialist ingredients, some high end food producers have started offering such things as smoked salt and smoked paprika. These items attract a premium price tag and contrary to popular belief are surprisingly easy to recreate yourself at home. Where smoked salt is concerned, the cardboard smoker comes into its own. Trying to smoke salt in a stainless steel cold smoker can sometimes be problematic especially with the moisture produced from the combustion process while generating smoke. This added moisture will help turn your precious sea salt into a pool of brine over time. Using the cardboard smoker, the chances of this happening are considerably reduced. Although salt isn't strictly hygroscopic it does have a tendency to absorb moisture that happens to be present in the atmosphere. Although I have no scientific evidence to prove my theory, my experience suggests the cardboard smoker acts to stabilise the humidity inside the smoker limiting the amount of moisture available for the salt to absorb. The same appears to be true for paprika. It's fair to say the same effect seems to be true for wooden smokers in that the fabric of the smoker acts to stabilise the moisture content of the smoke within the smoker.

The cardboard smoker is a very neat little smoker which I use and demonstrate regularly on my food smoking courses. It's environmentally sound too because when it reaches the end of its life it's not too expensive to replace and you can compost it or recycle the cardboard through your waste collection service. This use of a second hand cardboard box provides a good second existence for the cardboard box and, if the one I'm using is anything to go by, can last for two years or more if looked after properly.

garden food smoker

If, like me, you want to smoke food on a regular basis and you'd like something a little more permanent you could choose to construct your own garden food smoker. I first designed this food smoker after some inspirational writings from a gentleman called Keith Erlandson who authored what can only be described as a seminal work on food smoking and curing which has remained in print since it was first published back in the seventies (1977). In his book he describes with the aid of rudimentary diagrams different smoker layouts from which my design was born.

The design is a mix of both style and functionality and has been locally adapted over the years by those purchasing the plans to accommodate a large burn tray under the smoke spreader as an alternative to the remote smoke source, and different door designs. I first launched this design on the internet in September 2009 and since then I have sold many hundred of copies of the plans. Occasionally I receive emails and pictures from fellow food smokers who have taken the time to build from my original plans. It is truly inspirational to see these pictures which proudly show off their smoker working on various foods and it's also interesting to see some of the modifications that have been made to the drawings to suit their individual circumstances.

My design uses a feather-edged pressure-treated timber slat for the sides of the smoker. Similar to that used on fence panels. Over time this stuff moves and makes discrete vents in the side of the smoker. I don't mind this because it looks good in a garden setting. Any smoke escaping from the sides of the smoker can be plugged using silicone sealant but I think it only adds to its aesthetic qualities and charm if you can see wisps of smoke drifting around when it's in use.

I'm often asked about the use of treated wood in this smoker and my answer is simple. Because this is a cold smoker and the temperatures inside never reach above 30°C there is not going to be any interplay between the food and the preservatives within the wood or the silicone sealant. In addition to this fact, all the food smoked inside this smoker is on food grade stainless steel cake racks. Before using the smoker it is important to allow it to operate without food for about twelve hours to season the inside. This will ensure that any odours from the wood are eradicated. I do this for any smoker I use from new and it is accepted practice.

The original plans as they have been reproduced here in the book are detailed and while every care has been taken to reproduce them for your enjoyment you may prefer a larger format to work with should you choose to build the cold smoker. If that is the case, just send me an email to the address below and I'll email you a copy of the plans in PDF format and you can bathe yourself in fine detail until the cows come home.

The complete set of cold smoker drawings; construct your own cold smoker and enjoy the delights of fresh smoked fish and meat done the way you like it. The plans are easy to follow with full instructions. There is email support from info@coldsmoking.co.uk for sorting out any assembly or construction issues you may have. Please note, all dimensions are in millimetres.

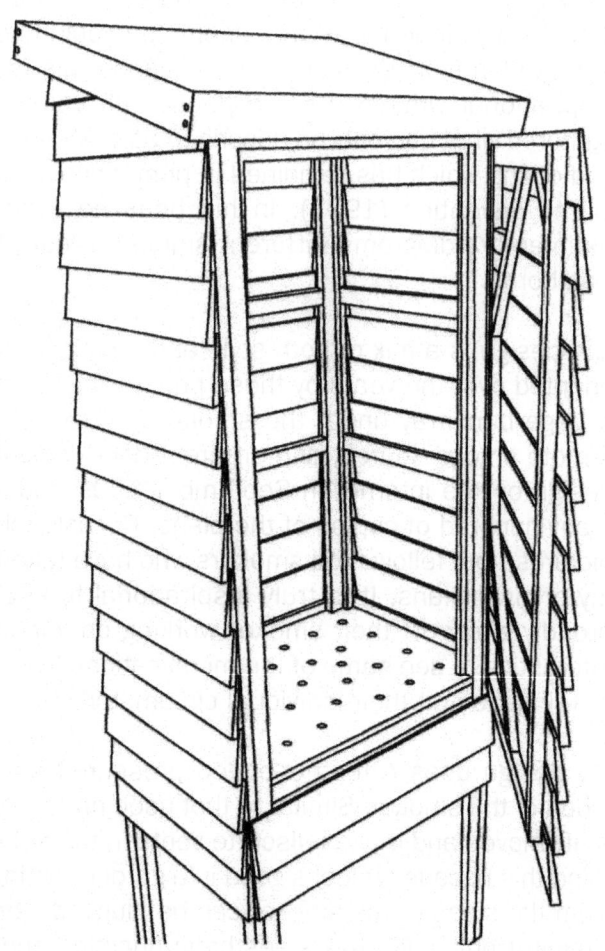

fig 28: the garden food smoker

To build this smoker you will need the following materials:

32 metres x 18mm x 32mm treated softwood batten (framing plus door)
32 metres x 100mm x 12mm feather edge board (cladding plus door)
3 metres x 48 x 20mm untreated, planed soft wood (roof)
wood glue,
1 x box 25mm panel pins
2 x 150mm black steel hinges (door)
1 sq. metre of mineral felt
1 x box mineral felt nails
12 x No 10 x 25mm galvanised wood screws (hinge fixing)
24 x No 10 x 30mm galvanised wood screws (roof fixing)
10 x No 10 x 40mm galvanised wood screws (side to back joining)
4 x No 8 x 20mm non-shanked galvanised wood screws (smoke pipe connector)
1 x 100mm standard plastic ducting connector plate (smoke pipe to smoker floor connection)
1 x door handle
2 x spring catches complete with screws (door)
4.5 metres x 12.5mm diameter hard wood dowel
4 x standard stainless steel cake racks.
1 x tube of silicone sealant
1 x 600mm x 900mm welded steel mesh 13mm gauge (shavings basket)
1 x standard galvanised dustbin style incinerator with lid
2.5 or 3 x M Flexible aluminium ducting
1 x 2400 x 1200 sheet of 12.5mm ply (floor, smoke spreader and roof)

tools

screwdrivers
hammer
wood saw
tape measure
carpenter's pencil
3mm drill bit
25mm wood bit (smoke spreader)
jig saw (smoker floor)
electric drill or hand drill
sharp knife plus spare blades
mastic gun
staple gun and a good supply of staples (I used the longer staples and tapped them home with a hammer)
large flat surface for setting out

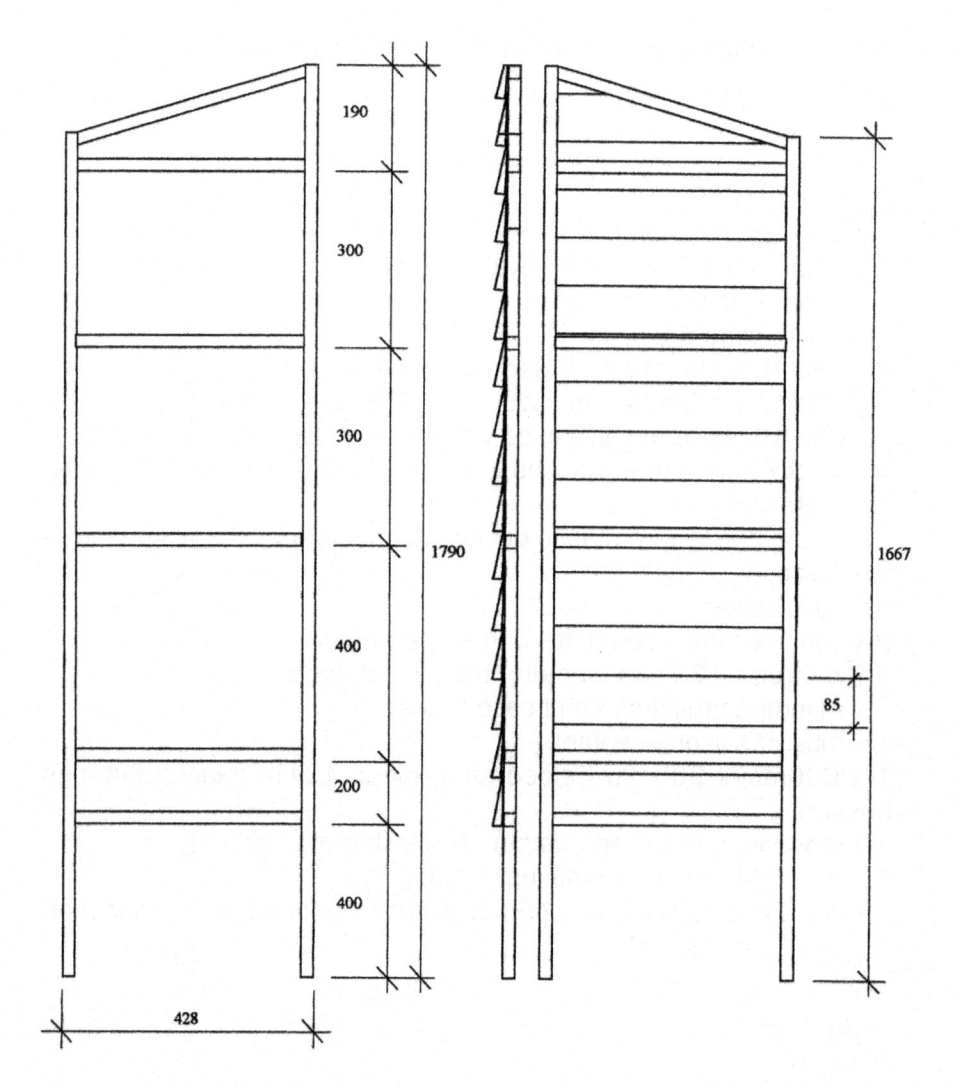

fig 29: the smoker sides

smoker sides

The sides of the cold smoker are constructed from 18mm x 32mm treated softwood battens stapled and glued in accordance with fig 29. The two sides are mirror images of each other and are clad with 100mm x 12mm feather edge (shiplap) sawn treated softwood. The side cladding is arranged with an overlap of 15mm. It's important to note that the dimensions of sawn timber vary slightly so it's worth arranging the boards first, adjusting the gaps to achieve a uniform look before fixing them in their final position. The sawn timber typically has slight inaccuracies in its overall dimensions and therefore all measurements taken from the sawn timber should be checked for accuracy and adjusted to suit.

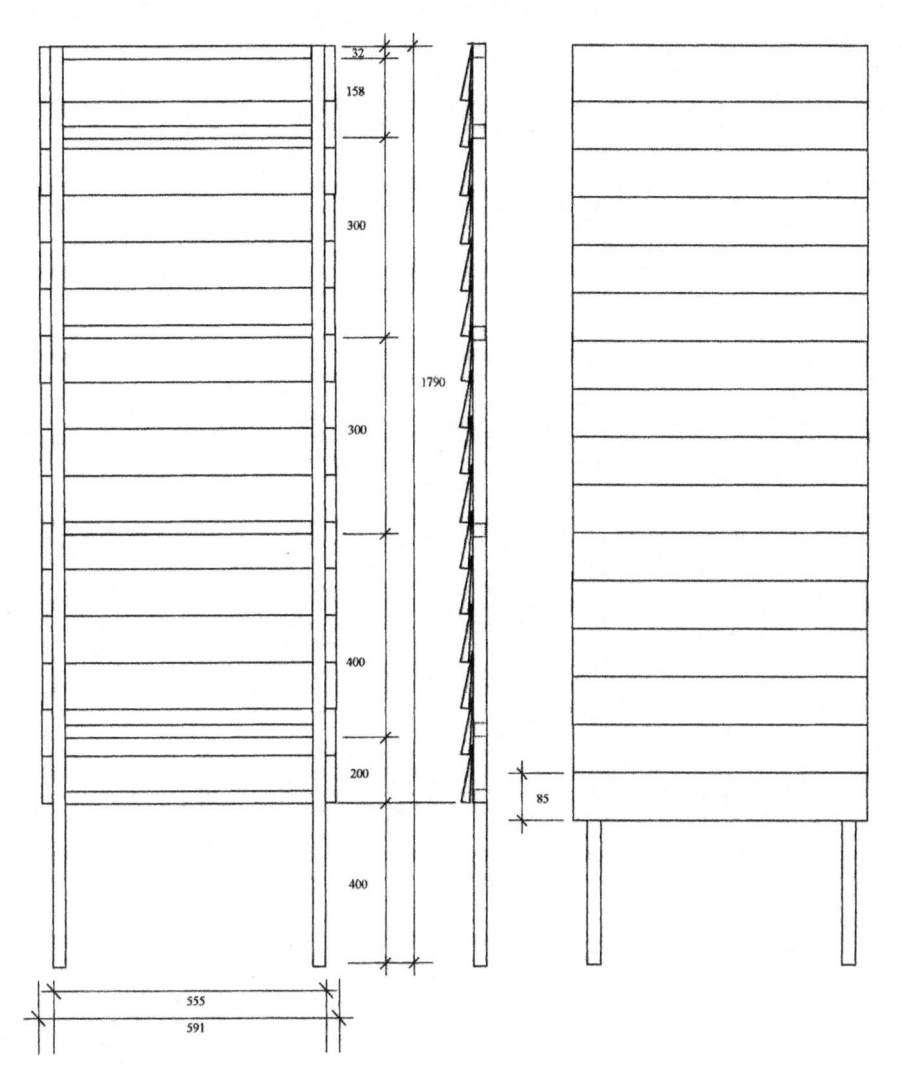

fig 30: the smoker back panel assembly

smoker back panel

The back and side elevations of the smoker are clad in 100mm x 12mm treated feather edge. There is a small overlap between each feather edge board (15mm approx.) to allow water run off. This overlap also serves to allow sealing between each overlapped joint. Typically, a thin line of silicone sealant applied from the inside face will provide a suitable seal allowing for the natural movement of the timber frame over time. Ultimately, this will prevent smoke from escaping and make your smoker more efficient.

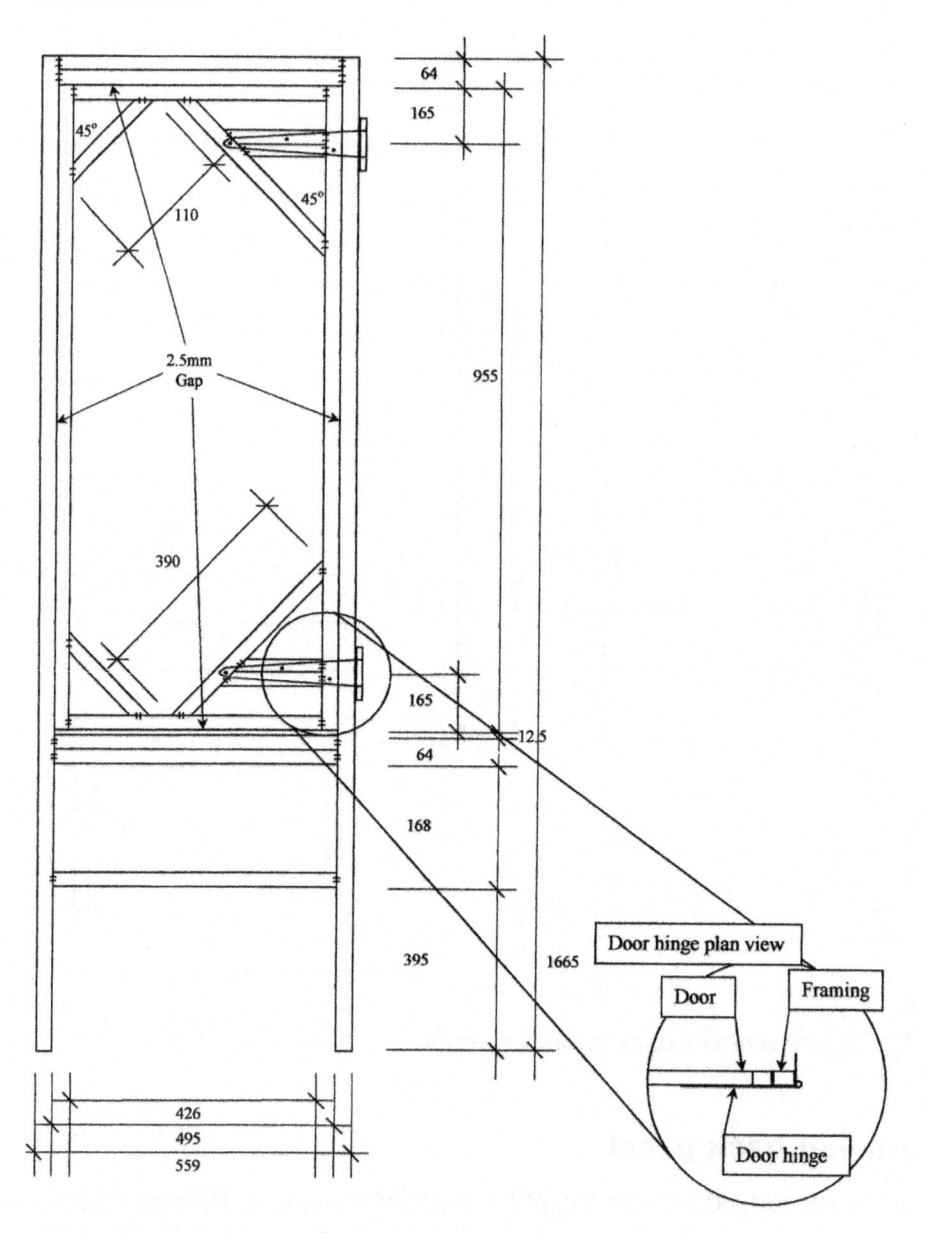

fig 31: the smoker door and front assembly

98　*food smoking* **L I L I**

smoker door and front assembly

The door and frame assemblies make up the main structures for the front of the cold smoker and are constructed from treated sawn timber (18mm X 32mm), glued and stapled as per fig 32. Cut and assemble all the pieces of the frame and door on a flat surface before gluing and stapling them together. Ensure the door is assembled and glued first so you have the finished dimensions to assemble the frame around. Check that the pieces are square before arranging the frame around the door structure.

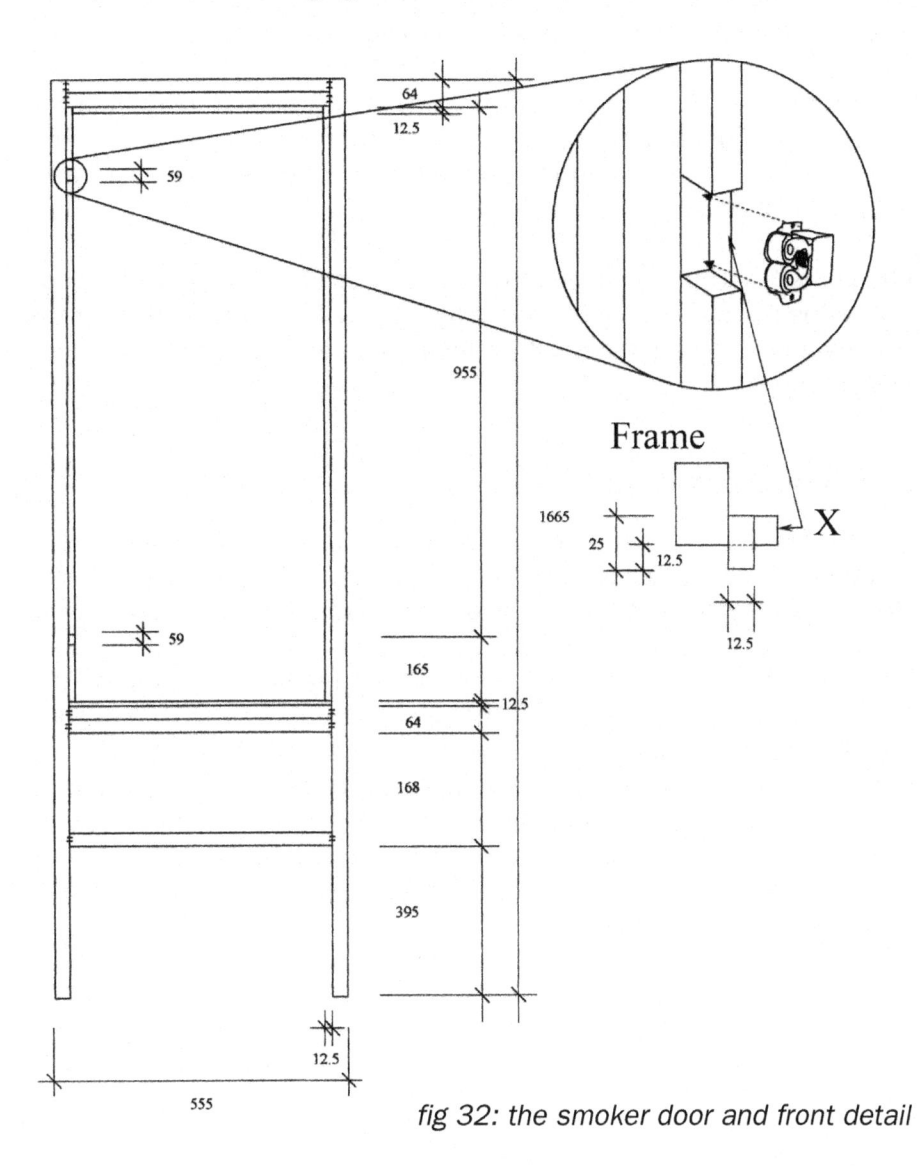

fig 32: the smoker door and front detail

Glue and staple the frame around the door ensuring the door and frame remain separate. Note the double top and bottom rail on the front framing. This double top and bottom rail is there to add strength to the frame.

The feather edge board forming part of the opening door should be fixed to the door frame only. Ensure that you maintain the same overlap as the sides of the smoker so when the cold smoker is finally assembled, all the overlaps are at the same level. This is mainly to achieve a uniform aesthetic look for the cold smoker and disguises the door.

important: the gap between the bottom of the door framing and the bottom rail is designed to accommodate the front edge of the smoke spreader. The gap between the door edges and the surrounding frame is 2.5mm on all surfaces.

Attach the 2 x 150 mm hinges to the door using 3 No 10 x 20mm wood screws as per fig 31 ensuring the hinge is positioned correctly over the hinge support rails and correctly oriented as detailed in the door hinge plan view.

door and front detail

The door frame forms an integral part of the front of the smoker and is designed to accommodate the door. This is clad with feather edge boards to conceal the door and to make it look the same as the sides and back.

The frame only requires 2 x 100mm x 12mm feather edge boards. The first is set square with the bottom edge of the lower rail. The second board sits 85mm above the first board giving a 15mm overlap. The top edge of the second board should just cover the lower of the two battens which are located at the front below the smoke spreader. These boards can be secured by staple and glue or nailed if preferred. X indicates where there is a double depth piece of door jamb to accommodate the door-closing spring catch.

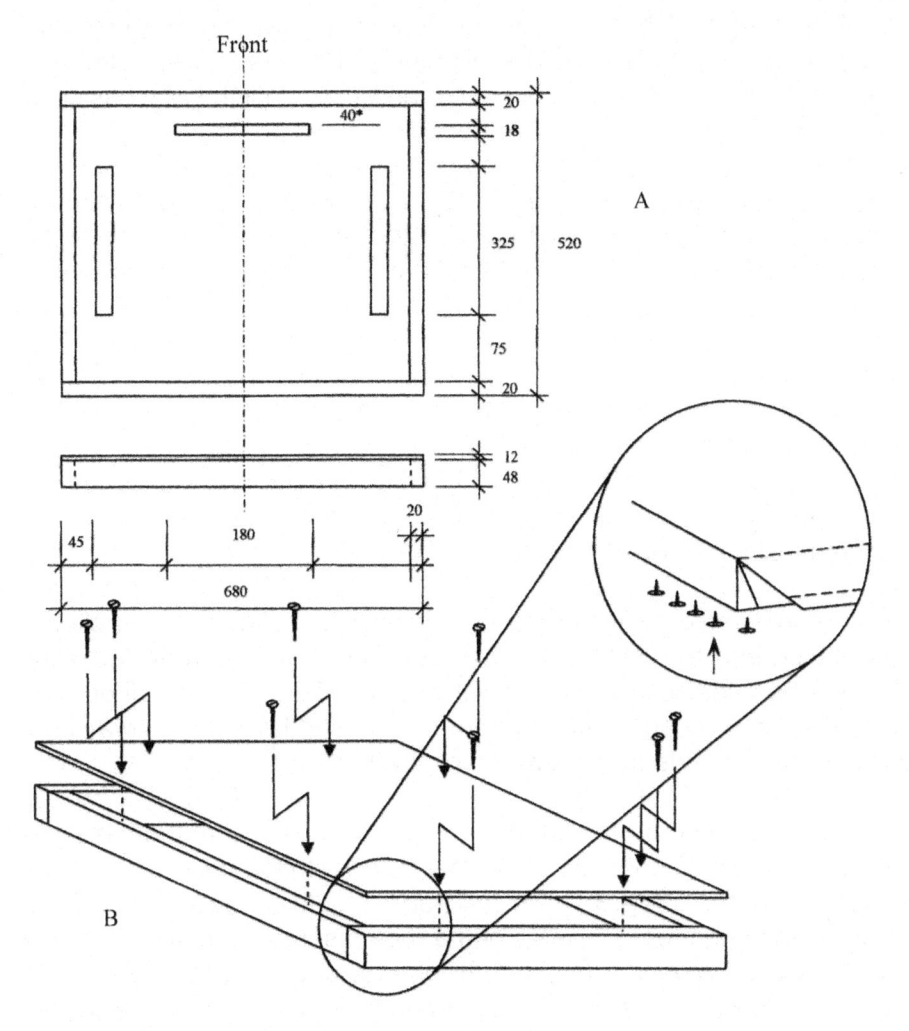

fig 33: the smoker roof frame assembly

roof frame assembly

The main roof frame is made from 48mm x 20mm planed softwood. The roof panel is made from 12mm ply and is held to the roof frame with 8 x No 10 x 30mm galvanised wood screws and PVA wood glue.

Construction of the main components begins with cutting the individual pieces to length 2 x 480mm and 2 x 680mm. Lay the cut timber lengths on a flat surface as shown in fig 33 'A'. Apply PVA wood glue to the ends of the two shorter lengths of roof framing and assemble. Check for square

L I L I food smoking

by taking diagonal (corner to corner) measurements, ensuring the same measurements for each of the diagonals. Hold the assembled roof structure in place with clamps or staples and leave until the glue has dried.

Cut the 12mm ply sheet to fit the dimensions of the roof (680mm x 520mm). Apply PVA wood glue to the top edges of the roof frame in preparation for fitting the roof panel. Set the roof panel on top of the framing and secure with 8 x No 10 x 30mm galvanised wood screws as shown in fig 33 'B'.

Because the roof is designed with a slope, it is important for it to sit squarely on top of the framing. If the roof sits too far forward there is a danger it could foul the door as it opens. To achieve this, 3 lengths of 32mm x 18mm treated timber should be positioned and secured to the underside of the 12mm ply roof. The side positioning strips can be secured using PVA wood glue.

tip: It is advisable to fit the front positioning strip after the smoker is assembled and the mineral felt has been fitted on the roof. Mark the position from inside the smoker with the roof fitted and the door open ensuring the two don't foul. The roof can be slid backwards away from the door or forwards to achieve the desired fit.

To ensure a weatherproof finish, the roof should be covered with mineral felt secured to the underside of the roof frame with felt nails, see mineral felt corner detail in fig 33. The felt nails should be spaced at 30mm between their centres. The edge of the roof assembly is quite sharp and there could be a danger of the roof felt cracking or becoming weak in this area. To overcome this it is acceptable to cover the roof with thin card or newspaper to soften the edge. This also makes replacing the felt easy as it won't become attached over time to the wooden roof structure.

floor and smoke spreader assembly

The floor and smoke spreader are both constructed from 12.5mm ply board. The smoke inlet hole in the floor is located in the centre of the floor. To find the centre of the floor draw 2 diagonal lines connecting opposite corners and where the two lines bisect will be the centre of the floor. Cut out a 100mm diameter hole using a jig saw. The holes in the smoke spreader are 25 mm in diameter.

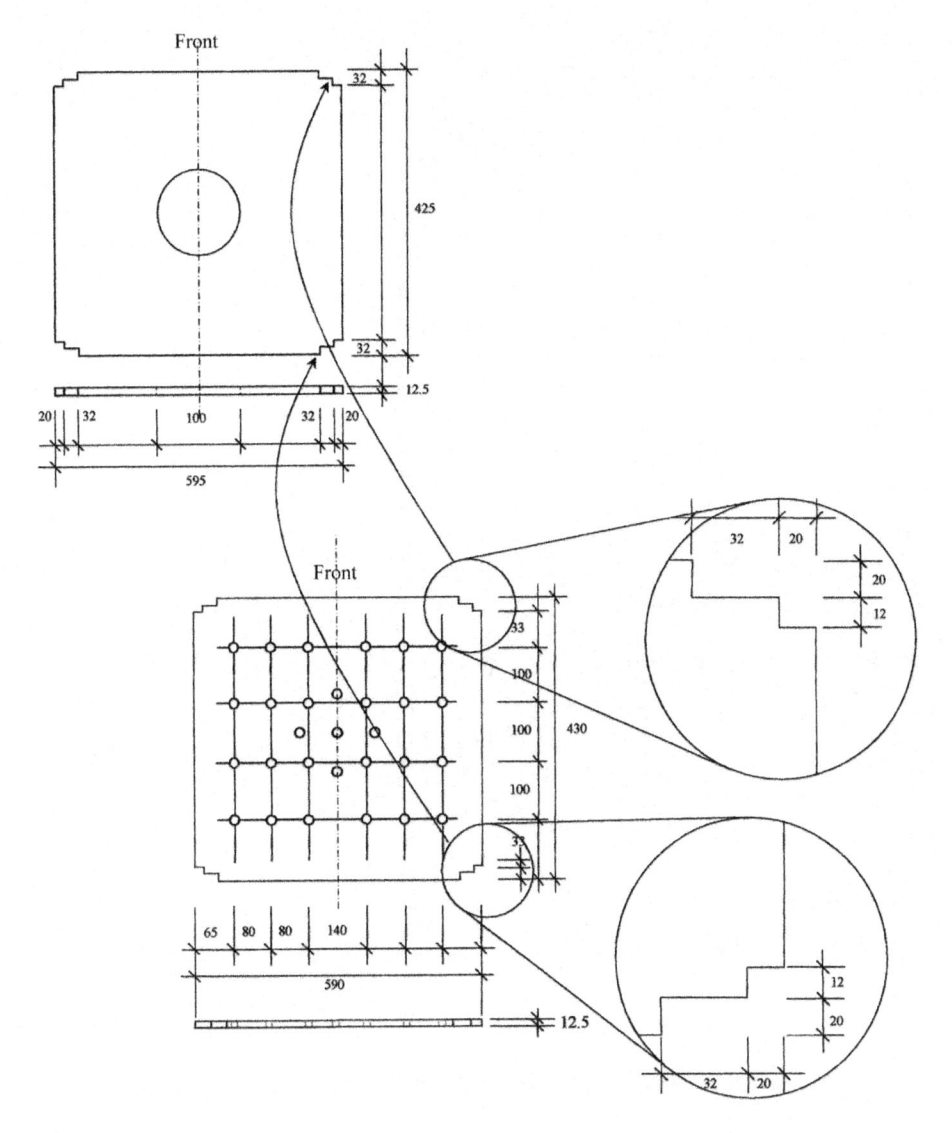

fig 34: the smoker floor and smoker spreader assembly

The corner details (shown enlarged in fig 34) on both the floor and the smoke spreader are the same. As both are symmetrical the detail can be mirrored for both sides of each piece.

LILI *food smoking* 103

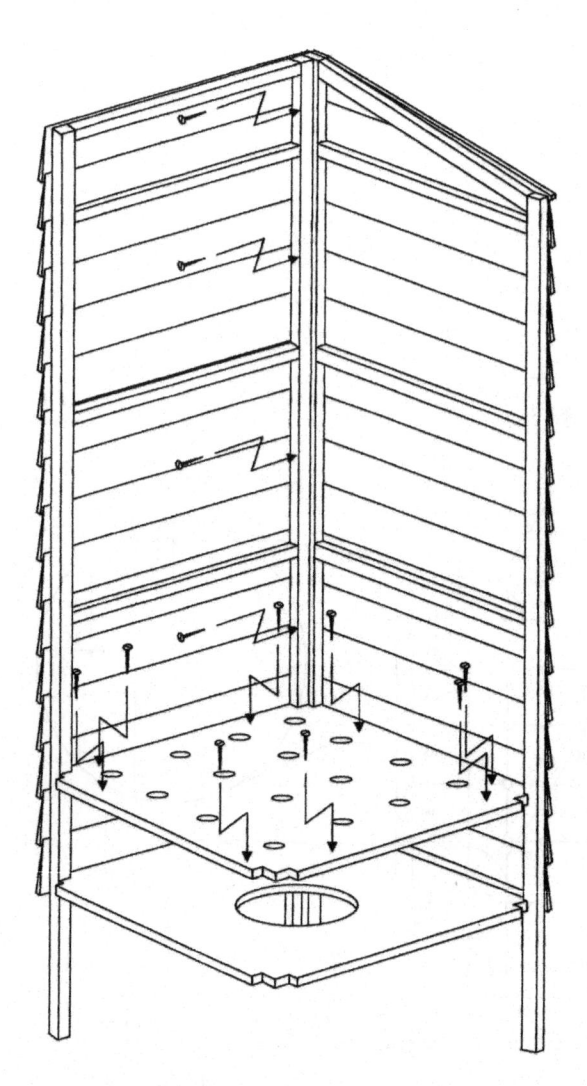

fig 35: the smoker back and side assembly

assembling the side, back, floor and smoke spreader

Loosely assemble the back panel and the right hand side panel and secure with 5 x No 10 x 40mm wood screws. To make this part of the assembly as easy as possible, pre-drill the 5 fixing holes using a 3mm drill bit.

Before fitting the floor & smoke spreader, fit the left hand side of the smoker to the back panel using 5 x No. 10 x 40mm wood screws in the same way as the right hand side panel. (Fig 35 shows this side removed for clarity.)

The floor of the cold smoker sits on the bottom support rail of the smoker sides and back. Secure the floor of the cold smoker to the back and sides of the smoker using 2 x No.10 x 30mm wood screws on each straight edge.

The smoke spreader sits on the second support rail above the floor panel. Before securing into position, apply PVA wood glue to the side and back rails, position the smoke spreader and secure with 2 No 10 x 30mm wood screws for both side rails and the back.

important note: Fit the floor of the smoker before fitting the smoke spreader.

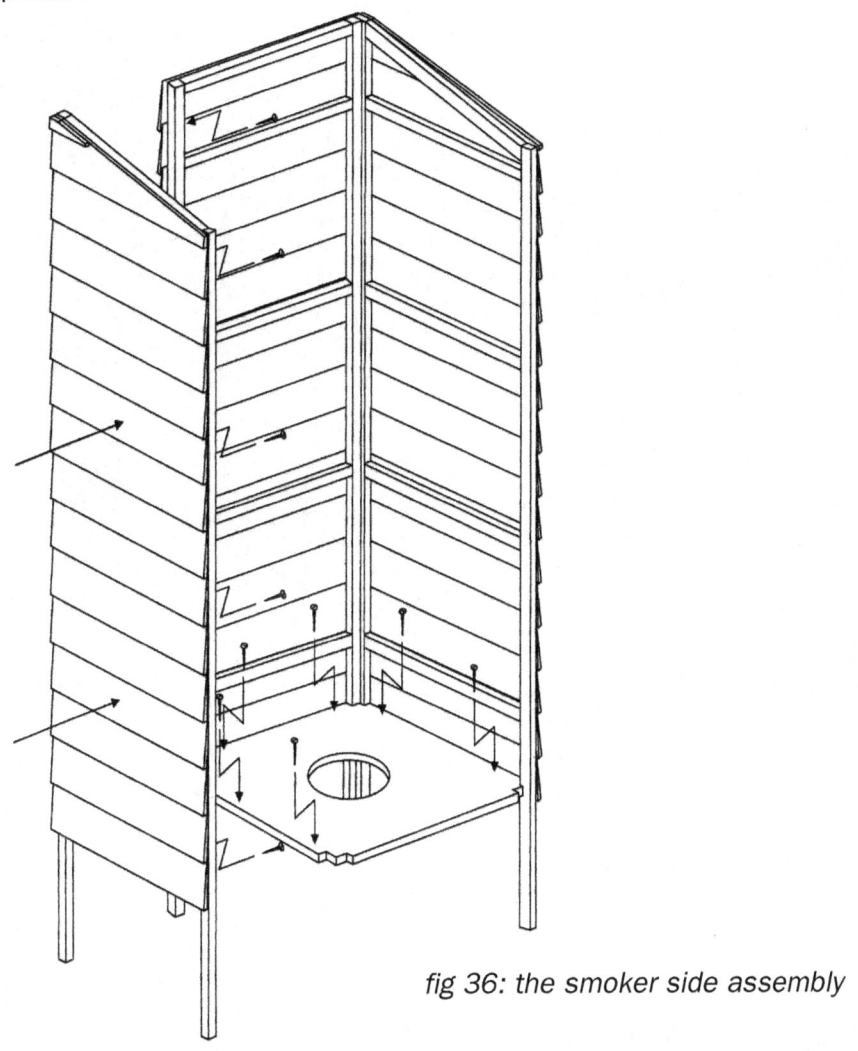

fig 36: the smoker side assembly

side assembly

Assemble the left hand side panel in the same way as the right hand panel using 5 x No 10 x 40mm wood screws. Use PVA wood glue on all joints.

Once the side panels are secured to the back panel secure the smoker floor to the sides and rear panel with 2 x No 10 x 25mm wood screws for each side. Again, use PVA wood glue on all joints.

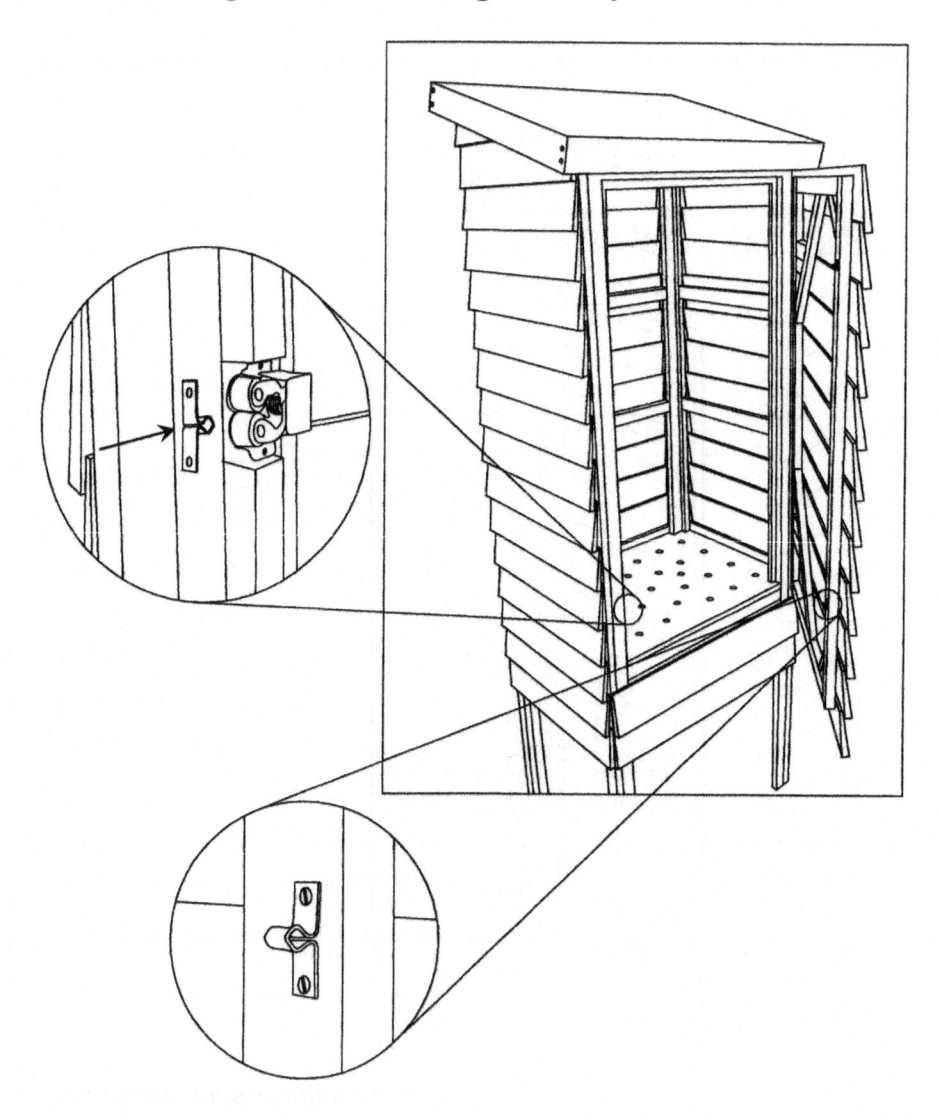

fig 37: the smoker assembly door catch details

door furniture

To ensure the door remains closed while the cold smoker is in operation, the door needs two sprung roller catches to be located on the door and frame as indicated in fig 37.

These catches are in two parts. The spring rollers are secured to the door frame and the clasp is screwed into the door.

Fig 37 shows the completed body of the smoker with the roof resting loosely on top of the body of the smoker. The supporting dowels and racks aren't installed yet as they are added during the final stage of assembly. This cold smoker is not fitted with a damper to control the smoke but rather uses a passive method of damping to allow the smoke to naturally leak from the gaps between the top framing and the roof structure. If using a remote smoke source the use of a damper on the smoke source may be necessary.

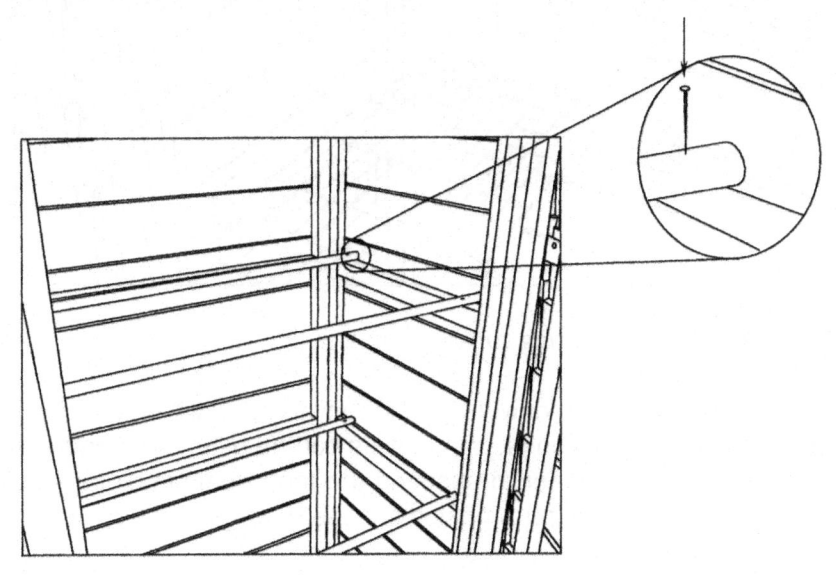

fig 38: the smoker supporting dowels

fitting the rack supporting dowels

To support the racks the smoker will need to have two 12.5mm dowels installed on each support rail as shown in fig 38. To fit the dowels they first have to be cut to size. Loosely fit the dowels on the support beam and place your wire rack on top of the dowels. Ensure the dowels are on the outside of the wire rack's stands. The space between them can be gauged before finally securing the dowels to the support rail with a single panel pin on each side.

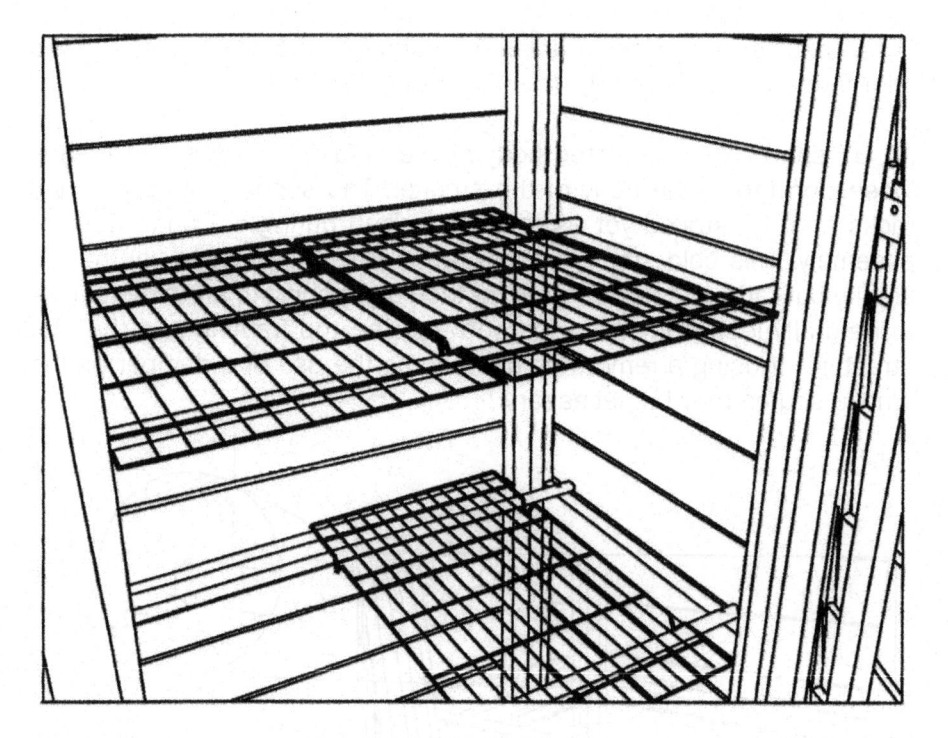

fig 39: the smoker supporting racks

The racks sit loosely on the dowels without any fixings; two on the upper rails and two on the lower ones. The dowels can be used independently without the racks if you prefer to suspend the food from stainless steel hooks. The racks are ideal for smoking cheese or large sides of fish.

Fig 40 shows 4 dowels installed on the uppermost support rail. They are installed in the same way as the dowels on lower rails (with a single panel pin) and can be accessed with the roof removed.

The 4 dowels installed this high in the cold smoker provide the ideal place to hang fish, meat and sausages.

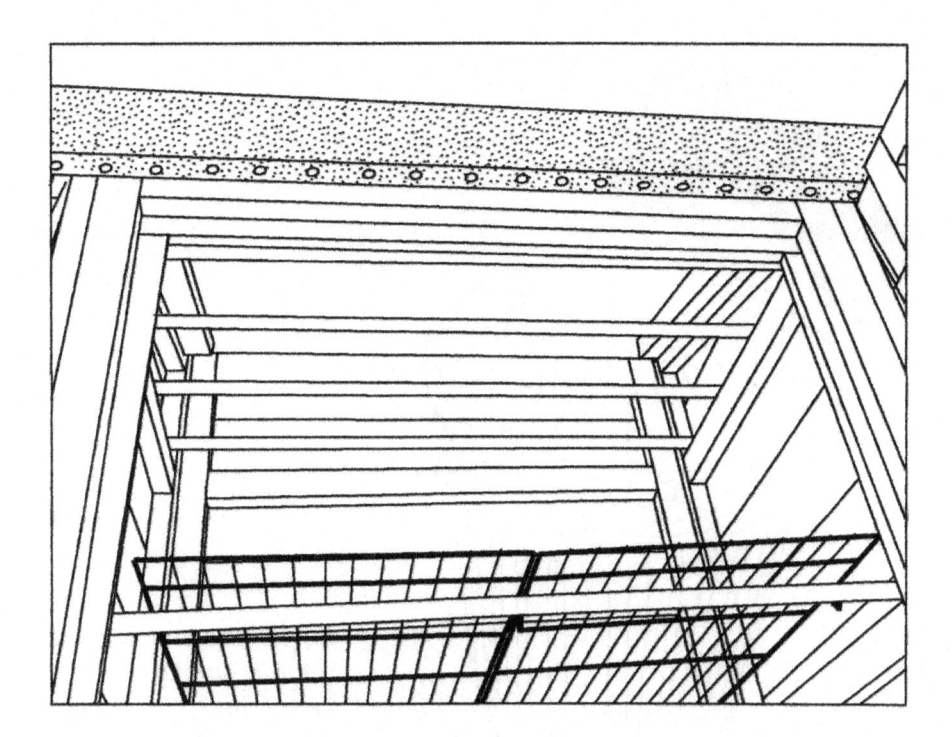

fig 40: the smoker high level dowel location

the smoke generator

The smoke generator is simply a modified garden incinerator and can be purchased from most hardware stores. The only modification required for smoke production is the sawdust basket.

The sawdust basket is constructed from welded sheet mesh 600mm x 900mm (13mm mesh size). The basket's dimensions are 240mm diameter x 500mm in length.

To construct the basket: form the mesh into a cylinder with a diameter of approximately 240mm. Secure the basket with sufficient wire ties twisted through the mesh where the mesh overlaps on the edge of the cylinder. Once secured, the base can be fabricated by making a series of small vertical cuts approximately 100mm in length and spaced approximately 50mm apart at one end of the cylinder. These cuts allow the mesh to be folded into the centre to form a base.

fig 41: the smoker remote smoke generator

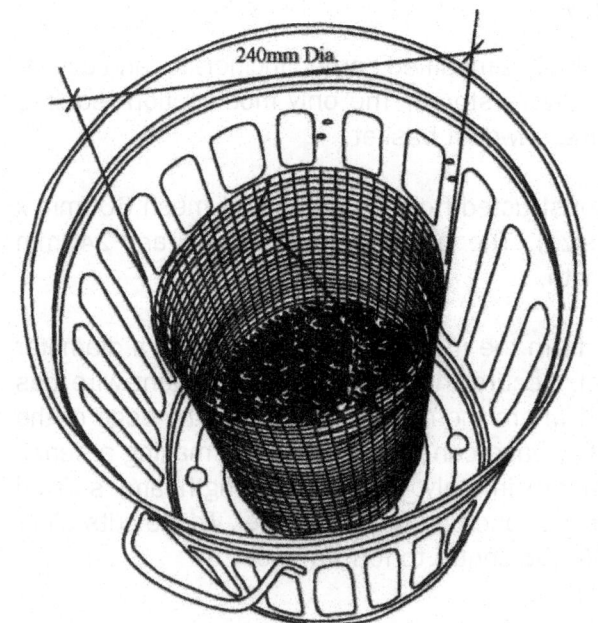

fig 42: the smoker sawdust basket

110 food smoking **L I L I**

The base is secured in the same way as the sides with a series of small wire ties twisted through the mesh where it overlaps.

To finish the basket a small metal pie tray should be placed at the base to prevent losing the sawdust through the bottom and a wire handle can be attached to the top of the basket to ease removal of the basket from the incinerator.

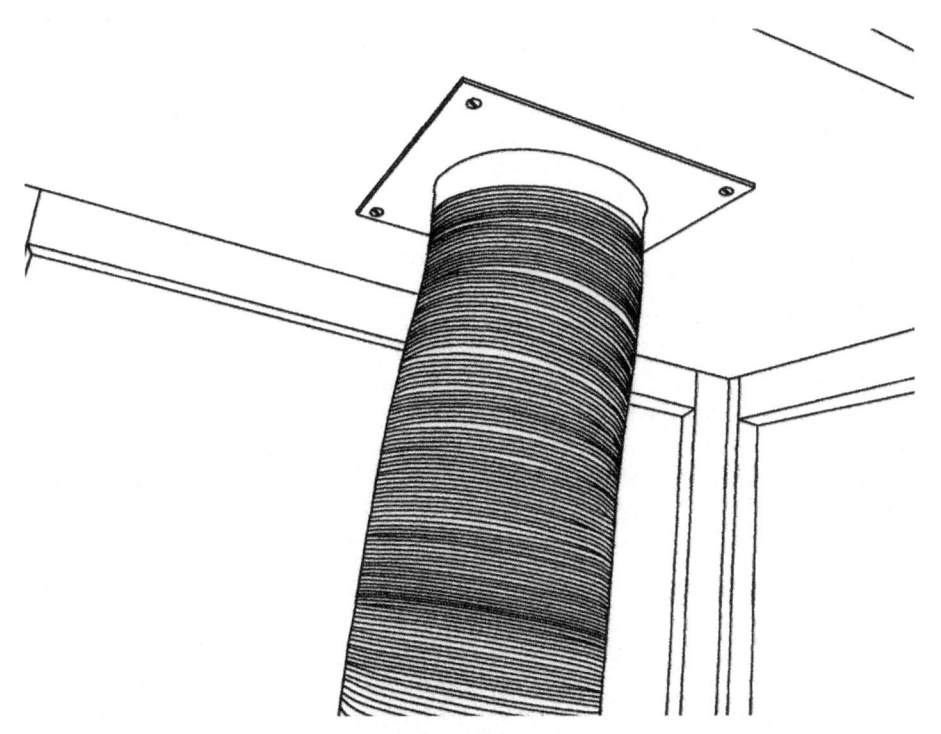

fig 43: the smoker remote smoke pipe

The smoke tube is simply 100mm x 2.5m of flexible aluminium ducting fixed to the underside of the floor of the cold smoker with a standard connector plate.

Thread the connector plate over the end of the smoke tube. The end of the smoke tube should be cut around the circumference at regular intervals to allow the ends to be splayed out. When the connector plate is fixed in position to the underside of the smoker floor the splayed edges of the smoke tube will be sandwiched between the connector plate and the floor of the smoker.

When attaching the smoke pipe ensure you apply silicone sealant between the connector plate and the floor of the cold smoker. Secure with 4 x non shanked wood screws of around 25mm in length.

If you wish to dispense with the remote smoke generator in favour of a dust burn tray or other tray-based smoke generator this can be used directly inside the smoking cabinet providing it is placed on a metal tray.

improvised hot smoker

roasting tray method

Improvising a hot smoker can be a cost effective way of hot smoking small quantities of food without breaking the bank.

This method employs two roasting trays, one with a raised rack, barbeque perforated foil tray and a couple of bulldog clips. The setup for this smoker is very simple using one of the roasting trays as a lid with the bulldog clips to secure the lips of the trays together. I have achieved consistently good results using this method and it is very similar in principle to more expensive versions of stovetop smokers and gives equally good, if not better, results.

The setup is as follows. One of the roasting trays forms the base of the smoker. The perforated foil barbeque tray sits flat in the base. The raised roasting rack sits on top of the foil tray. The lid of the smoker is the other roasting rack and the bulldog clips secure the two halves of the hot smoker together. I've used this method to smoke trout, venison, steak and duck breasts and I'll explain how to do this a little later on in the book, see page 145.

To use this improvised hot smoker couldn't be easier. The amount of wood chips or dust you use it will largely depend on the size of your roasting trays. For a regular-sized roasting tray I would use no more than a tablespoon of chips or dust. There is a tendency sometimes to use more chips or dust, but as this is an enclosed smoker you really do get a bang for your buck in terms of smoke. Because the environment in the smoker is completely closed, very little of the smoke escapes and therefore it makes extremely efficient use of the smoke it produces. Too much wood chip or dust and your food will taste of tar and will be completely unpalatable. If you use larger roasting trays, like turkey roasting trays, you may be able to get away with using a little more chip or dust, but I would suggest using no more than one and a half tablespoons. Don't be tempted to heap the tablespoon, just a gentle mound.

Using the smoker on a portable stove outside is the safest method of operation and will prevent smoke smells in the kitchen.

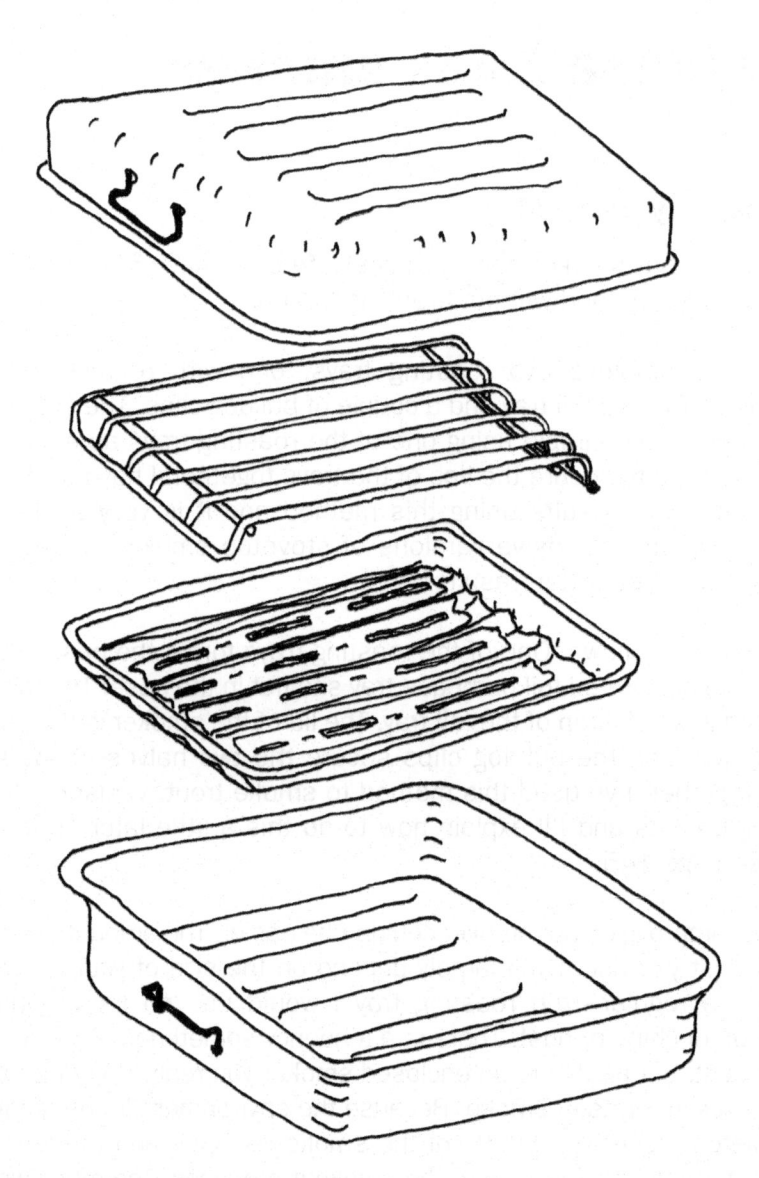

fig 44: improvised roasting tray hot smoker

I have used this smoker indoors on a stove with a good cooker hood extractor to remove the smoke and I was surprised to find that it didn't really produce much smoke at all. This is mainly due to the fact the smoker is sealed with the bulldog clips. Stovetop smokers are used in many commercial kitchens across the world. Using them in this environment with the correct training is a very safe thing to do. Using an improvised smoker on the other hand is a completely different matter.

Because the roasting trays are held together with bulldog clips and the side handles of the roasting trays are not really designed to be held without oven gloves great care should be taken when using this method. Safety is really important and I would always recommend using oven gloves to remove the bulldog clips and separate the roasting trays.

Cameron stovetop smoker

As the name suggests this is a purpose built stovetop smoker. Made from stainless steel it is essentially the same as the bottom half of the improvised hot smoker with the addition of a sliding lid.

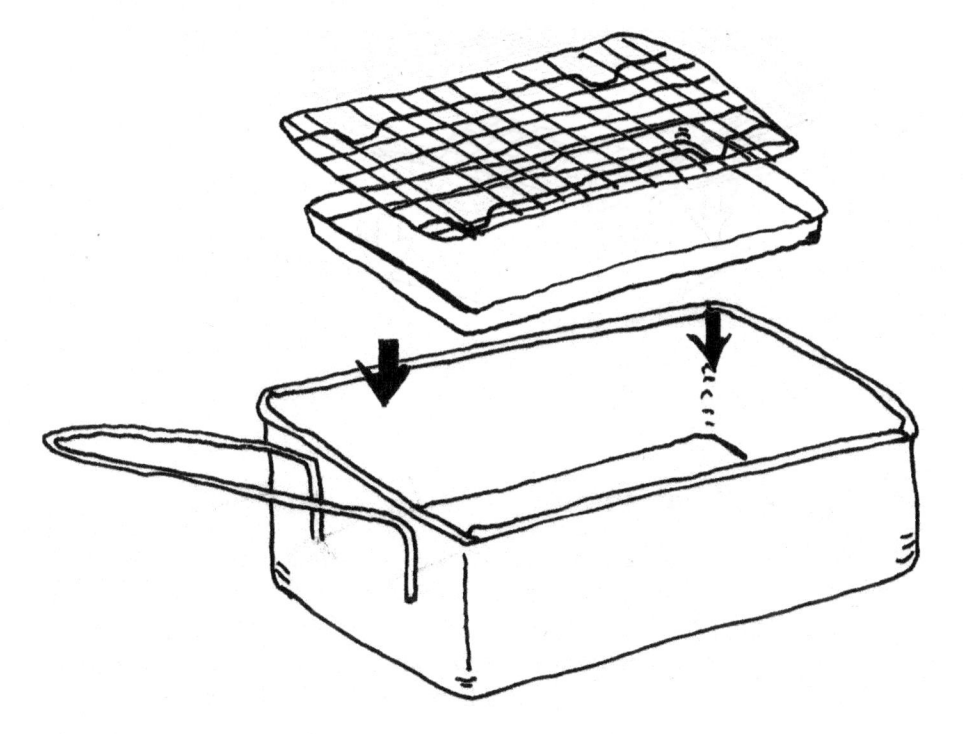

fig 45: Cameron mini smoker

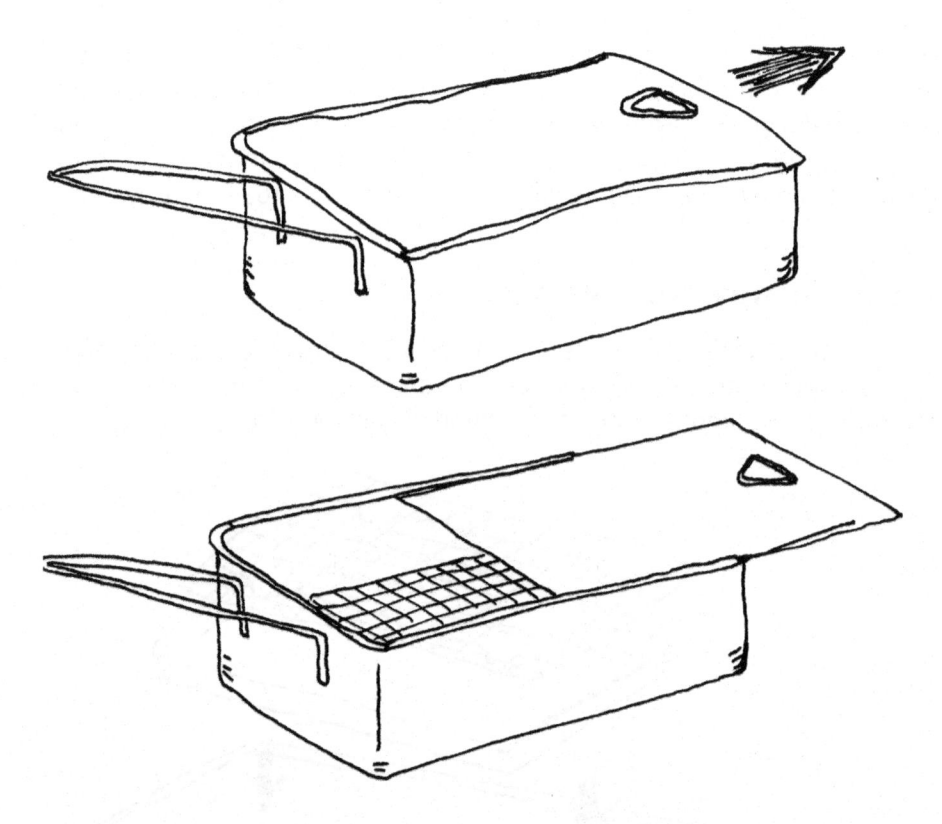

fig 46: Cameron mini smoker with lid

barbeque grill hot smoker

Millions of people across the globe love to smoke food using their barbeque. This section of the book will be a little like teaching your granny to suck eggs for the experienced barbeque smoker but for those just starting out there is a really simple way of achieving lovely smoked barbequed food without the use of a kettle barbeque with a lid (or other designs with lids, of which there are many). I have managed to adapt a simple charcoal barbeque to act as a hot smoker. This is easy to do. I would just like to qualify that statement by saying that my particular charcoal barbeque doesn't have a lid but nevertheless the adaptations I have made are too simple and make it very easy to achieve. Fig 47 shows clearly that my barbeque has three sides and just by placing an inverted roasting dish on top of the grill it's possible to create a small smoke reservoir under which the food can enjoy a good smoking.

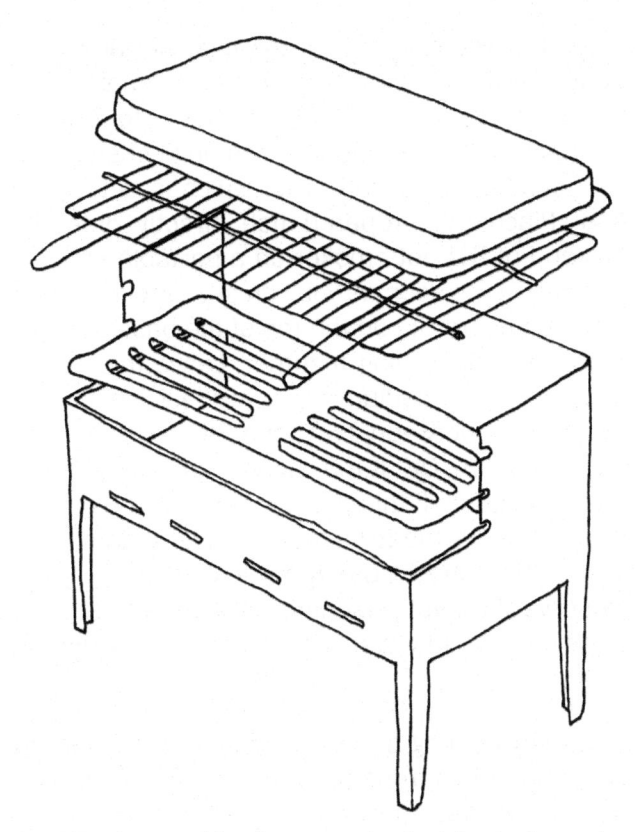

fig 47: charcoal barbeque adapted for hot smoke

This method is just as effective using aluminium foil to trap the smoke and I have produced spectacular hickory smoked chicken using both methods. By generating the smoke by adding some soaked wood chip directly on the coals or by placing a foil packet containing wood chip onto the charcoal it's really very easy to enjoy excellent smoked food from a simple lidless barbeque. If you do have a lid on your barbeque you're already there.

hot smoked trout

Use an improvised hot smoker to produce some delicious hot smoked trout and find out how easy it is to do.

Carry out the basic set up for the improvised roasting tray hot smoker but before placing the foil tray in the base of the roasting tray select your desired wood chips or dust and place a tablespoonful of them in the centre of the roasting tray. Put the foil tray in place and lay the roasting rack on top of the foil tray. Now you're ready for the fish. Gut and rinse two 1lb (400g) trout. The gut cavity can sometimes close on smaller fish. One method of adding a little extra to your smoked trout is to insert a couple of sprigs of tarragon or some small slices of lemon nestled neatly inside the gut cavity. This imparts a subtle flavour which is detectable amongst the smokiness. Place the prepared fish directly onto the roasting rack of the smoker. Put the hot smoker on a portable stove in the open air and turn the heat on. As soon as you can see smoke coming from the wood, place the roasting tray lid on the top of the base and use the bulldog clips to secure the whole thing together. Leave this for 20 minutes. The stove should be on a medium heat. In ideal conditions, where the outside temperature is between 16°C and 30°C, 20 minutes cooking and smoking time should be OK. It may need a little adjustment according to local weather conditions. If this procedure was to be carried out in a commercial kitchen indoors the 20 minutes would be ample. If there is a breeze outside, or the temperature is particularly low, protect the stove in order to preserve the heat ensuring that all the heat from the stove goes into the smoker. It may also be necessary to lengthen the cooking time.

This method cooks the trout by heating the surrounding atmosphere to a point where the moisture in the fish turns to steam. At the same time the heat from the stove will pyrolyse the wood chips through indirect heating producing hot smoke. Initially the temperature of this smoker will exceed 130°C but once there is sufficient steam from the fish the temperature will stabilise at around boiling point (100°C).

When the cooking time is up turn off the heat, remove the bulldog clips and the lid making sure to avoid the smoke and heat plume. The fish should be cooked. This can be tested if you have a heat probe by inserting it into the thickest part of the fish. If the temperature is above 74°C the fish will be cooked and safe to eat, if not pop it back on the stove for a few minutes more.

Remove the fish from the smoker and discard the skin as this takes the majority of the smoke and can be a little strong. The flesh should retain a mild smoky flavour which tastes wonderful hot or cold. Cooking trout using with this method means the fish can be allowed to cool to room temperature with the skin on and placed in the fridge for a day to allow the flavour to develop further. It can then be used as part of a cold salad or turned into smoked trout pâté.

smoking fruits, nuts, vegetables and cheese

Throughout this book much has been made of the virtues of smoking meat and fish. In truth this is only part of the story as there are some wonderful examples of smoked vegetables out there and it's worth just having a go to see what you can come up with. While cold smoking meat and fish in the early days was for the most part undertaken to preserve the food, the addition of smoke to vegetables seems to have evolved out of our passion for the taste of smoked food and our insatiable appetite to try new things by mixing it up a bit.

In most cases, smoking vegetables (either hot or cold) can be achieved with relative ease and with some quite stunning results. There is usually no more preparation required than chopping the food up into manageable chunks to get it into the smoker. Some vegetables take the smoke well raw and just require the addition of some cold smoke for a couple of hours while others can take the smoke while undergoing a cooking process (hot smoking). Either way the results can be extremely rewarding and if you are a vegetarian wishing to get your hands busy with some food smoking you can be just as involved as the omnivores of this world.

I've compiled a list of the most popular smoked vegetables and the methods for producing them. For ease, I have included spices, herbs, rice, beans and pulses here too. The list is not an exhaustive one and I'm sure there are some vegetables that I have missed. I can assure you, if I've missed them out it's because I haven't tried them yet!

smoked fruit

Most fruits can be smoked and it's really up to your individual taste where you take this. I have smoked apples and orange and lemon peel which I have later dried and preserved for use in cakes. Smoked dried citrus peel is particularly nice and very easy to produce. Simply place the peel on an open wire rack in the cold smoker and leave to smoke gently for four to six hours. Preparation of the peel is important as one should remove the pith from the peel before smoking. It's funny, but the only way we were able to swear in front of our parents as children was when we were eating fruit and telling each other in loud voices that we were taking the pith off before we ate it! Oh how we laughed.

Raisins cold smoked and used in fudge produce wonderful points of flavour and work well with the sweetness of the fudge. This combination also works well with smoked almonds or cashews which we will cover later in this chapter. The raisins are simply scattered onto a baking tray and cold smoked for four to six hours.

Figs can take the smoke really well and can be cold smoked for around four hours. I find that fresh figs don't work as well as dried figs but that is my personal preference. You may wish to try smoking fresh figs for yourself to see if they're more your taste. I find dried smoked figs chopped finely onto breakfast muesli or granola adds a nice little smoky something to the start of your day.

smoked tomatoes

Tomatoes and smoke were made for each other and cold smoked for around four to hours make a lovely addition to any salad or casserole. I prefer to roast my tomatoes before smoking them on a baking tray, then storing them in an airtight jar with oil. With fresh tomatoes one can just halve them and place them in the smoker raw for the same length of time. The only point here is they will not last as long as the roasted tomatoes. Roasted or sun-dried tomatoes in oil can be sourced quite easily and make lovely anti-pasta. Simply draining the oil from the tomatoes, spreading them out on a baking tray and cold smoking them for about four hours produces a wonderful adjunct to any salad or starter. If you dry your own tomatoes, just brush with vegetable or olive oil before smoking them. Once they've smoked, the tomatoes will keep for about a month or two if stored in oil. Place the smoked tomatoes in either vegetable or olive oil and leave them to mature. If you're storing them in oil make sure the oil covers the tomatoes completely to maintain their freshness for as long as possible. Not only will you have lovely mellow smoked tomatoes but the oil which has now taken on the smoke flavours can be used to make a smoky tomato and mustard salad dressing.

smoked nuts

Smoked almonds, cashews, pecans and hazelnuts make a creative nibble or festive treat and are really easy to make. The way I make smoked nuts depends largely on whether I'm going to store them for a later date or eat them straight away, either way the initial preparation method is the same. The first step is to roast the nuts. This is essential as it begins to develop the flavour of the nut. You can smoke peanuts but remember if they are roasted already this step can be missed out. To roast the nuts scatter them on a shallow baking tray, place in the oven for 10 minutes at 180°C in a fan oven. Increase this temperature by 10°C if you are not using a fan oven. Be very careful when roasting nuts as they can burn in the blink of an eye. Almonds and cashews are particularly difficult to get just right. Remove from the oven and allow them to cool down.

While they are cooling melt some oil or butter in a pan. This is the part in the method that changes depending on whether you are eating them straight away or storing them for a while. I coat the nuts in butter if eating straight away and vegetable oil if keeping them for a while. The nuts keep for about three months if coated in oil but only a few days if coated in butter as it has a tendency to go rancid after about five days. Incidentally if your smoked nuts last five days, you're obviously doing something wrong. When the butter has melted, remove the heat from the pan and add the nuts. Coat the nuts with the melted oil or butter until they are well coated and shiny. I then add a mixture of sugar and salt in the ratio of four parts sugar to one part salt and add this to the pan, stirring until the mixture has coated the nuts completely. The butter or oil acts to keep the sugar/salt mix on the nuts. The nuts are now ready for the smoker. They can be spread out on a baking tray or placed in a vegetable steamer tray and cold smoked for four to six hours. For a quicker version I hot smoke the nuts in my improvised hot smoker for about five minutes. This is just to get the smoke into the nuts quickly. When the nuts come out of the smoker allow them to stand for about an hour to cool and mellow before tasting. I have to say these are very moreish so if you're preparing them for later do try and exercise some restraint by only tasting a few.

I like to experiment with different woods when smoking nuts and I love the idea of hazel smoked hazelnuts. Or pecan smoked pecans. I've even considered harvesting the husks from peanuts in their shells to experiment with these. I think that's for another book perhaps. Some suggest smoking with almond gives a bitter unpleasant finish but this is something I haven't had the opportunity to test out for myself. In conclusion smoked nuts are very simple, store well and can be packaged up to make an excellent foodie gift for a loved one. Whilst on the subject of nuts, it's worth collecting your festive nut shells to use when smoking on a barbeque as these can add an exotic twist to your food. Shells from walnut, hazelnut and pecan are perfectly acceptable to use.

smoked peppers and chillies

Either dried or fresh red or green peppers can be cold smoked for anything from four to six hours and go extremely well in salads and omelettes. Dried peppers can benefit from being lightly brushed with oil beforehand to help the smoke stick to them. Dried peppers can also take the smoke for a lot longer, twelve to twenty-four hours if your taste is for a heartier smoke flavour.

smoked garlic

One of the most popular smoked vegetables I'm asked about is garlic. Smoking garlic is too easy for words as it just sits in the smoker until it's done. It really doesn't need any preparation in its bulb form so it makes a great introductory vegetable for the novice to cut their teeth on.

The use of smoked garlic often stimulates quite a bit of debate as it's pointed out quite quickly that when cold smoked, the smoke only goes on the outer layers penetrating a negligible amount and having little or no discernible effect on the taste of the actual garlic clove. This of course is true. The skin surrounding the garlic can be almost impervious to anything, providing a very effective barrier to the smoke. This is not such a bad thing as there are several layers of papery outer skin on a bulb of garlic that absorb smoke quite well. These outer layers are effectively the key to a smoky flavour when roasting other vegetables or meat in the oven as the flavour from the skin can be imparted onto the other vegetables or meat, especially if they are initially roasted in a foil package. Place a bulb of heavily smoked garlic in a roast chicken and see how well it imparts flavour to the bird. Some have suggested that the whole concept of cold smoked garlic is a bit of a con and a matter of style over substance but as I explained earlier the garlic bulb should be used to flavour other things. If you want to smoke the actual garlic clove itself then you'd be better off hot smoking it. Nevertheless, a plate of smoked garlic is an attractive thing and not just for the eyes.

The other way I like to smoke garlic is by lightly roasting it in individual cloves. To prepare: skin three bulbs of garlic down to the clove ensuring you remove all traces of the skin from the clove. Place the cloves on a baking tray and roast in the oven until they are just beginning to soften. Don't over roast as this will make the garlic bitter. Allow the garlic to cool on the baking tray, brush with either vegetable or olive oil and place the tray in the cold smoker for four to six hours. The cloves can be stored in a glass jar topped up with oil and can be used for soups, stews or as a direct replacement for roasted garlic.

smoked paprika

I'm often asked how to smoke paprika. I've found the best way is to spread some powder evenly over the surface of a baking tray, placing it in the top of a cold smoker and leaving it to smoke for six to eight hours. Every hour, turn the paprika with a fork to expose more of the unsmoked powder underneath. I find that because paprika has a strong flavour anyway, smoking it with a robust smoke like oak or hickory complements it and works well with the flavour of the paprika. It's best to store smoked paprika in a sealed container so it maintains its smoky aroma and flavour. Used in making chorizo, stews and meat rubs for barbequing this is a versatile ingredient which is very easy to produce.

smoked olives

I find olives really moreish. Having once eaten an olive straight from a tree many moons ago I really appreciate the alchemy that goes into the brining of these little darlings and makes them what they are. Smoking olives is very easy and is as simple as placing them on a shallow baking tray and putting them in the cold smoker for about four to six hours. The slight oiliness of the skins takes on the smoke really well and they are lovely eaten on their own or as part of a mixed salad.

smoked oils

Some smoked oils are lovely as dressing for salads or for tasting with bread. Really fine olive oil in my opinion shouldn't be smoked as its grassy or peppery notes are such that they can stand on their own. Regular olive oil can take the smoke really well as the oil and smoke are miscible with each other and the flavours penetrate through the oil very quickly. To smoke olive oil, use a roasting dish or some other pan with a large surface area and some depth so it can contain the oil without spilling. Cold smoke it for four to six hours, stirring the oil every hour. Re-bottle the oil and use on salads and in dressings. There is a commercial producer of smoked rape seed oil that smokes the seed before pressing. The pressing itself releases the oil which passes over the seed husk imparting the smoky flavour as the oil leaves the press. This is an elegant method as the oil is not exposed to air for a prolonged time.

There are other methods for smoking oil. Sprigs of fresh rosemary or thyme can be cold smoked for four to six hours and placed directly into the oil bottle, infusing both the flavour and aroma of the herbs and smoke into the oil at the same time. These smoked oils make a fantastic base ingredient for salad dressings and vinaigrettes or can be enjoyed on their own with some lovely fresh bread.

smoked rice, wheat, lentils, beans and pulses

All of these can be smoked to add character to the finished product and can be an excellent way of enhancing flavours. The smoking process is similar to paprika, see page 123, and the rice, wheat or lentils are placed on a baking tray and exposed to the smoke for about six to eight hours, turning them with a fork occasionally to expose the entire contents of the tray to the smoke. This won't preserve whatever you are smoking but should be seen more as adding a new flavour dimension to your dishes. It's advisable to smoke these ingredients before they are cooked as rice especially can cause problems with bacteria if left at ambient temperatures for any length of time once cooked. A great deal of enjoyment can be gained from experimenting with different wood combinations when smoking rice, wheat, legumes or pulses. Smoking rice with apple wood or herbs like rosemary and then preparing the rice as normal will add a delicate smoky flavour that complements the food you intend serving.

smoked tofu

Tofu is a soya bean curd which is formed into blocks and usually stored in water with traces of calcium sulphate which is used as a coagulant. Tofu is quite wet when it comes out of the packet and although it can be eaten straight away like that, it will need to be pressed to remove most of the water before smoking it. There are also firmer grades of tofu on the market which have already been pressed. Tofu takes on flavour very well and can be lightly seasoned with salt before pressing. Tofu can be cold smoked for four to six hours but in order to develop a good colour and fuller flavour it can be smoked for a lot longer. Eight to twelve hours smoking will greatly develop the flavour and colour. I suggest using a strong wood like oak or hickory to achieve the desired colour and depth of flavour as tofu can be a little bland to start with. Tofu is a great flavour sponge and takes on most flavours really well and that goes for smoke too.

smoked cheese

Cheese can be smoked simply by exposure to smoke. It requires no elaborate preparation other than to place it on a wire rack in the smoker. I have included here some basic steps in preparing cheese for the smoker but these are no more than common sense. There is such a wide variety of cheeses on the market that knowing which ones to smoke really does come down to personal choice. There is however a general rule of thumb that I follow and that is simply if the cheese is particularly aromatic and has a very complex flavour and aroma, adding smoke to it can sometimes be a little pointless. Some blue cheeses for instance have a very distinctive nose and palate and the addition of smoke can be too much. Having said that Stilton does benefit from the addition of oak and some fruit woods smoke so for me to lay down any hard and fast rules would be a fool's folly as a great deal comes down to personal preference. Smoked cheese is a really rewarding way of taking a wonderful food to a completely different place. There are many different cheeses which work well with smoke and choosing a combination of wood smoke and cheese is a very satisfying endeavour.

preparation

Smoking cheese couldn't be easier. Simply place it on a rack in the cold smoker, choose your wood dust and leave it for a few hours to bathe in smoke and that's all there is to it. Personally I find that the cheese always tastes better the day after initial smoking as it has time to mellow. The only basic preparation I afford the cheese is to cut it into one or two centimetre strips before smoking. Simply, this increases the surface area which is exposed to the smoke allowing for quicker results and deeper penetration. Cheese does not need the same level of protection salt affords meat or fish in terms of restricting bacterial growth so there is no need to brine cheese before smoking. In any case, salt is used as part of its manufacturing process and adds nothing in the way of protection, only flavour.

Edam is my personal favourite as this takes on smoke really well. It always tastes better the following day and is wonderful melted onto a jacket potato. Edam smoked with apple or cherry wood is lovely and seems to develop a sweetness from the smoke which is quite noticeable.

Camembert and Brie take the smoke well and can take a little time to develop colour in their rind but when they do the results are excellent. I always smoke Camembert and Brie in the round. Smoking them on an open wire rack in cool conditions is no problem but beware when the temperature is in the 20s as you may end up with melted cheese on the base of your smoker. When the cheese is a little ripe and the temperature is in the 20s I smoke Camembert and Brie with their wrappers sitting underneath the cheese preventing any potential drips! Or I make a small foil tray for them to sit on. The same rules apply to goats cheese or any other cheese that is liable to melt easily or is a little on the ripe side. Some rindless goats' cheese is so soft it refuses to stay put on a wire rack for any length of time and will eventually fall through.

storage

Smoked cheese should ideally be stored in the fridge either wrapped in waxed paper, vacuum packed or in a plastic container. Smoked cheese will make your fridge smell if it is not wrapped up or sealed properly as will any smoked food. Try to avoid using foil as I have noticed a reaction between smoked cheese and aluminium foil which spoils the cheese and I have had to throw the cheese away. This is probably due to the acidity in the smoke reacting with the metal over time.

uses

Smoked cheese can be eaten as it is or grated in salads or over jacket potatoes. Simply put, smoked cheese can be a substitute in most recipes where cheese is required. Used as a tasty topping on a Shepherd's pie, in a cheese sauce or melted on toast this is one versatile, tasty ingredient. I have said this before but it's worth reiterating – you are only limited by your imagination when it comes to smoking cheese. There are literally thousands of different cheeses and many different woods to choose, the one limiting factor is most likely to be the time you have to experiment.

smoked salmon

Producing high quality home-smoked fish is becoming a popular activity for many home smokers. The growth of interest in organic food and many people's desire to understand what goes into producing their food has been the driving force in the unprecedented interest in this artisan craft.

I stated at the beginning of this book that I have written it as a practical guide to food smoking. By showing readers how to make a smoked product like smoked salmon I feel some may consider I'm wandering off course a little into the cook book territory. My thinking on this is simple; what's the point of building a smoker and having nothing to try out in it? Having said that, I wanted to choose something that is likely to give you pleasure from your smoker. Sorry if you are a vegetarian, there is much pleasure to be had from smoking vegetables and I have also included a few ideas to whet the appetite elsewhere but for me I consider smoked salmon to be a real winner for the home smoking enthusiast and therefore worthy of special attention here.

In earlier times, when smoking was primarily a form of food preservation, large amounts of salt and long smoking times were used to help preserve the fish. Nowadays fish are smoked more for flavour and appearance than for preservation. Today's lightly salted and smoked fish is not really considered to be a preserved product in the truest sense of the term; the amounts of salt and smoke used are NOT usually enough to prevent bacterial spoilage. Most food poisoning bacteria can and will grow under the conditions normally found in preparation and storage of smoked fish. *Clostridium botulinum*, the bacteria that may cause botulism, is the most harmful of these bacteria.

Making a safe smoked product whether at home or commercially requires a good understanding of the procedures and precautions needed to prevent food poisoning. The following paragraphs are really designed as a guide to these important precautions and explain why they must be followed to prepare safe, high quality smoked meat and fish.

Smoking food at home is an interesting pastime and can and does produce the most wonderful results from what are otherwise basic (but good) food ingredients. It never ceases to amaze me the reactions I get when I tell people I make my own smoked salmon, or when I tell them I smoke my own trout or cheese. There's an apparent childhood fascination about anything to do with fire and being able to control this primeval force to add value and taste to your food is a thing of true beauty. I still smile every time I walk from the cold smoker with sides of cherry- and oak-smoked salmon in a dill and brown sugar cure; and when I demonstrate these food smoking techniques on my courses and my delegates taste the results, their comments and the looks on their faces remains for me my primary motivation for showing people how to make smoked salmon and, of course, for writing this book.

key steps to making smoked salmon

Smoking salmon usually requires five steps in its production. This is not always the case when hot smoking as hot smoking food is usually only carried out for immediate consumption thus making the brining/salting stage unnecessary. The addition of salt when hot smoking is purely for taste and this can be achieved by dry salting or immersion in pre-mixed brine solution. A good example of hot smoked food which receives a salt treatment is the Arbroath Smokie. Remember, hot smoking is essentially a cooking process.

The five key steps for cold smoking salmon are:
- preparation
- salting
- drying
- smoking
- storage

Each step is critical to producing a good quality, safe product and it is important to follow the steps to minimise the potential for bacterial growth and food poisoning.

things to consider

Almost any fish or meat can be smoked. Fatty fish, such as salmon, can be brined and smoked much more easily than leaner varieties. Lean fish, such as grey mullet, sea bass or halibut are just as easy to smoke but it's worth noting the flesh can absorb salt very quickly, and it is easy to end up with a product which is far too salty for most tastes.

Only high quality fresh or frozen fish should be used for smoking. Using poor quality fish will produce a poor smoked product. Smoking will not disguise the fact you've used poor quality ingredients. Remember, you can only turn good food into great food.

When preparing salmon for smoking, it is important to keep the preparation area as clean as possible. Raw fish is considered a high risk product and should always be handled with the highest standards of food hygiene in mind. Keeping the work area, cutting boards and knives spotless is of the utmost importance but should not be overshadowed by the importance of personal hygiene standards. Keeping ones hands clean at all times and avoiding cross-contamination will go a long way in preventing bacterial growth and reduce the risk of food poisoning. Do not, under any circumstances, handle raw fish where the finished smoked product is kept. This could result in cross-contamination. Bacteria could be transferred from the raw salmon to the finished product and that would just not do.

Clean the salmon carefully to remove slime, blood and harmful bacteria that may be present on its surface. Then fillet or split the fish, leaving the skin on the fillet. Fillets of salmon vary in thickness along their length from only a fraction of an inch or a few millimetres at the tail end to around an inch or a couple of centimetres at the gill plates. With a little experience, dry salting a whole fillet can be achieved quite successfully by applying salt onto the surface of the salmon in direct proportion to the thickness of the fillet. More thickness, more salt is the general rule.

During preparation, the fish should be kept as cool as possible. This will help keep bacterial growth and spoilage to an absolute minimum. The ideal temperature for holding fish during the preparation stage is at or below 3°C. Home refrigerators are often 4°C or higher so do check the temperature with an appliance thermometer and adjust the controls as needed.

Another common problem with wild caught fish is parasites. Many fish contain tapeworms and nematodes that can survive some low salt brining and low temperature smoking methods like cold smoking. Ingestion of these parasites could possibly lead to serious health problems. These parasites can be destroyed by freezing the raw product at a temperature of -20°C or below for 24 hours, before salting and smoking, see *resources* page 179 for details.

When freezing the product in a home freezer, it may take several days to reach -20°C throughout the entire fish; the more food you put in the freezer at one time, and the thicker the pieces of food are, the longer it will take to freeze the food.

For hot smoked product (see *hot smoking*, page 36) the internal temperature of the fish should be raised to at least 70°C for two minutes in order to kill off any parasites. Temperatures in excess of 60°C are usually sufficient to kill off most parasites. Therefore, only fish intended for cold smoking needs to be frozen prior to processing especially as the temperatures involved in the cold smoking process are too low to kill off dangerous bacteria. It may seem like stating the obvious but always remember to wash your hands before and after handling food to avoid cross-contamination.

purchasing the fish

In this day and age truly wild salmon can be fairly difficult to source especially in areas far from their migratory path. For this reason and in the absence of wild-caught salmon, I prefer to source my salmon controversially from the mass market. It's likely that I could be subject to some criticism for this approach because I am fully aware of some of the issues around animal welfare standards for fish farms and the pollution some farmers have been responsible for. The standards of care have been reported as dire in the past and there are moves, especially in the US and EU, for salmon farmers to clean up their act. This problem is widespread for other species and other areas in the world and I'm aware that sea bass farmers in the Mediterranean have come under severe criticism for some of their practices in recent times. Having said all that there are some good operators out there and because the market demands a good quality, consistent supply, we can all enjoy this wonderful fish at a price most can afford. I have to say that without this ready source of consistently good quality fish I wouldn't have had the opportunities or depth of pocket to explore this wonderful pastime and pass my discoveries onto others in the way I have been able to.

For me, the handling of the fish before it gets to the customer is a key issue for discussion before we get onto the subject of turning it into smoked salmon. For most consumers I would guess they wouldn't really care too much about the handling of a fish providing it reached them in reasonable condition. Most customers' first reaction with fish is to give it the nose test. If it smells OK then that's usually enough to be going on with. Handling fish at the point of dispatch and until it reaches the customer is vitally important if you intend to use it for smoked salmon. Bruised fish can leave blemishes which do nothing for its appeal and speed up spoiling. When a salmon is dispatched it will start to spoil immediately. Once any living creature dies it immediately loses the ability to fight infection and starts to become overrun by bacteria from within its guts and its surface. The salmon should be gutted and frozen in the shortest possible time. Further damage can be sustained where the flakes of flesh are split apart in the raw product. On inspecting your salmon if you discover the flakes are coming apart after you have taken the fillets off the bone, this is a clear indication the fish has been handled roughly, especially soon after dispatch when rigor mortis has set in. Rigor mortis is essentially a gradual stiffening of the flesh after death and occurs in most creatures.

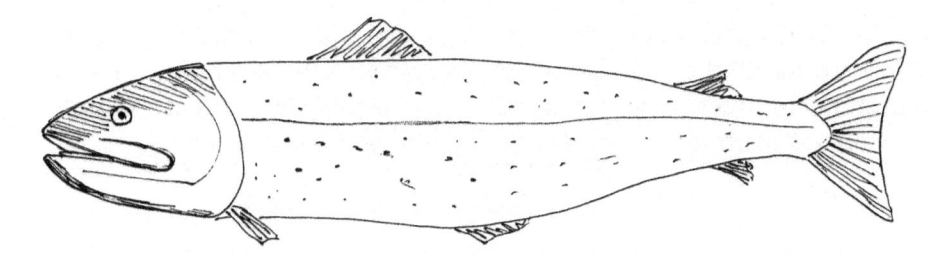

fig 48: salmon

knives

The type of knife to use for filleting is important. It should be slightly flexible and as a prerequisite it should have an extremely sharp, non-serrated blade long enough to be able to reach from the dorsal fin through the body of the salmon and out through the belly. This is important as it allows you to make the initial cuts to remove a fillet in one move while having the strength and rigidity to be able to make the initial cut through the skin, which can be quite tough.

To trim the salmon after it has been filleted you can use a small paring knife with a six or eight inch non-serrated blade. This is useful for cutting around the perimeter of the fillet to improve its look after you have taken the fillets off the bone.

The sharpness of the knife makes a big difference to the amount of effort it takes to remove a fillet and to make them as neat as possible; a sharp knife is essential. Follow the guidance in the *enjoy your hobby safely* chapter to make double sure, see page 13.

The fish tweezers are a standard bit of kit. Most good cook shops will stock these and there are loads to be sourced from the internet. My advice would be to go for a good quality stainless steel pair. The tweezers should grip firmly and they make the job of pin boning the salmon so much easier.

filleting

Before filleting the fish you will need to remove the guts. First, make a slit along the ventral (belly) side from the vent (anus) to the gill plates or lug bones at the back of the head. Discard the guts. With your finger break the membrane protecting the blood channel situated at the back of the gut cavity directly above the spine. This is best done under running water. There may be some veins in the belly walls of the gut cavity. These can be pierced and squeezed out to remove traces of blood but don't worry too much about these as you can remove these when taking out the rib bones later on in the process. The blood won't affect the taste but can detract from the appearance of the finished salmon.

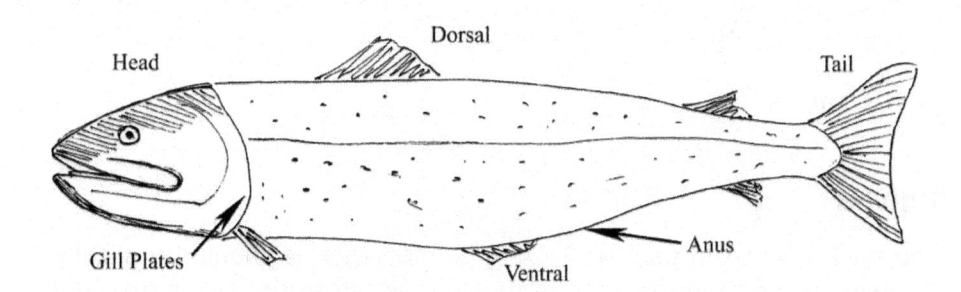

fig 49: basic salmon anatomy

To fillet the fish, lay it flat on your cutting board with the dorsal side towards you (gut cavity facing away from you). Make a cut towards the spine as close behind the gill plates as possible on what will be the fillet. When your cut reaches the spine; turn the knife through 90 degrees so the blade now faces down the length of the fillet towards the tail and lays parallel to the spine. When making the vertical cut behind the gill plates one can remove the head but it is not essential as it provides something to get hold of while taking the fillets off the bone.

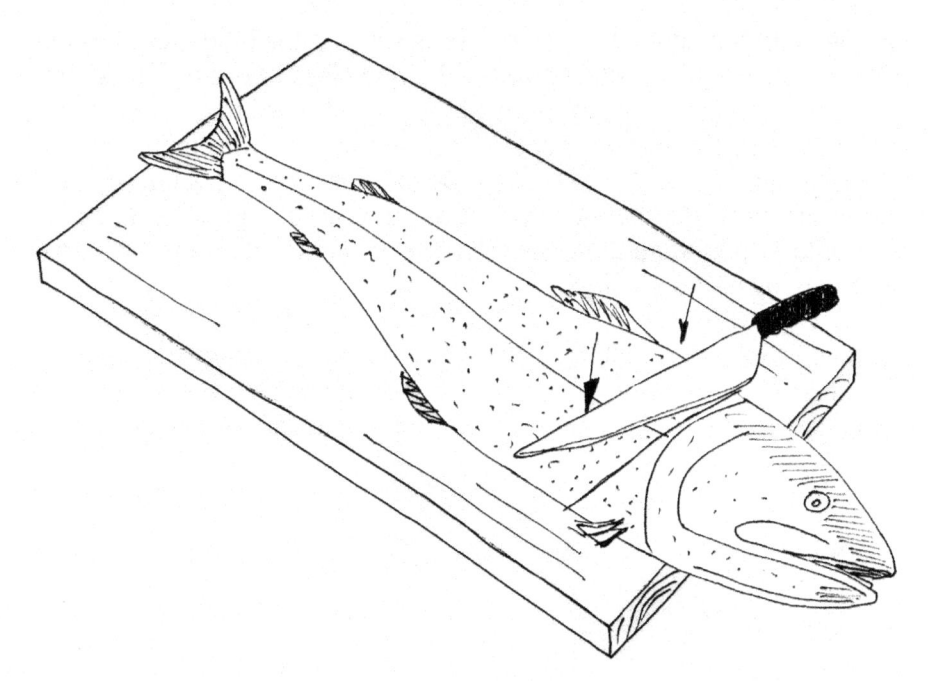

fig 50: filleting the salmon

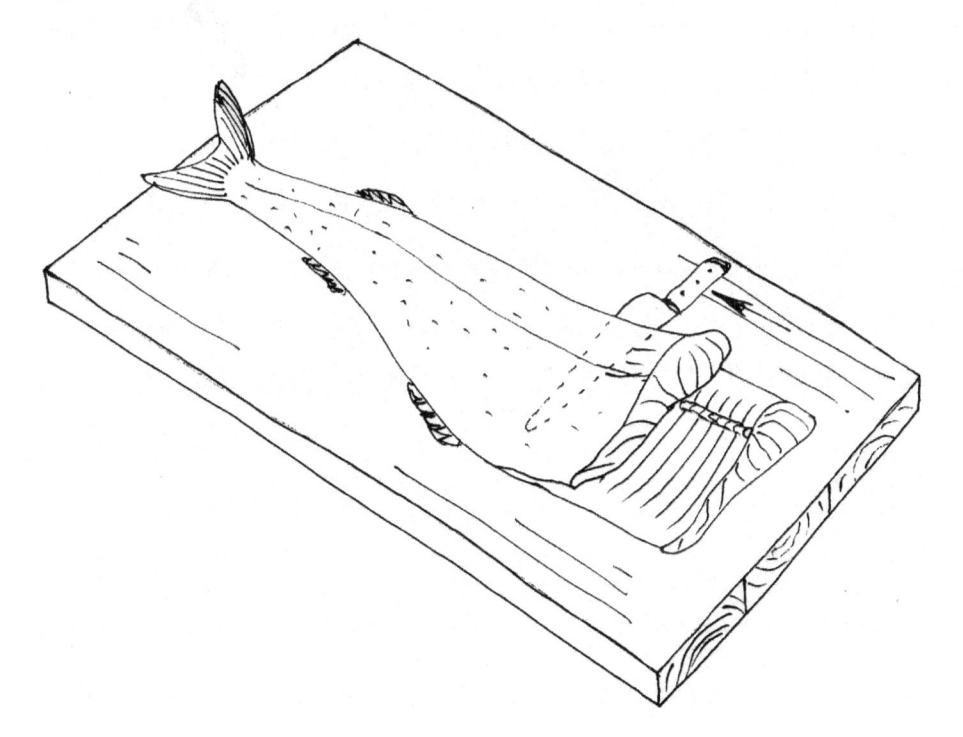

fig 51: removing the first fillet

With the knife flat against the spine, start running the blade towards the tail of the fish, initially cutting through the rib bones where they meet the spine. Keep the blade as flat to the spine and as close to the centre line of the salmon as possible to ensure you remove the maximum amount of flesh from the bone. Be careful as you cut past the dorsal fin, you may need to lift the knife slightly to negotiate this area. The same goes for the anal fin. Continue cutting towards the tail until you release the fillet from the body of the salmon.

To remove the second fillet, turn the fish over and repeat the process for the first fillet. Sometimes it can be a little tricky removing the second fillet as it's closer to the work surface and a little harder to judge.

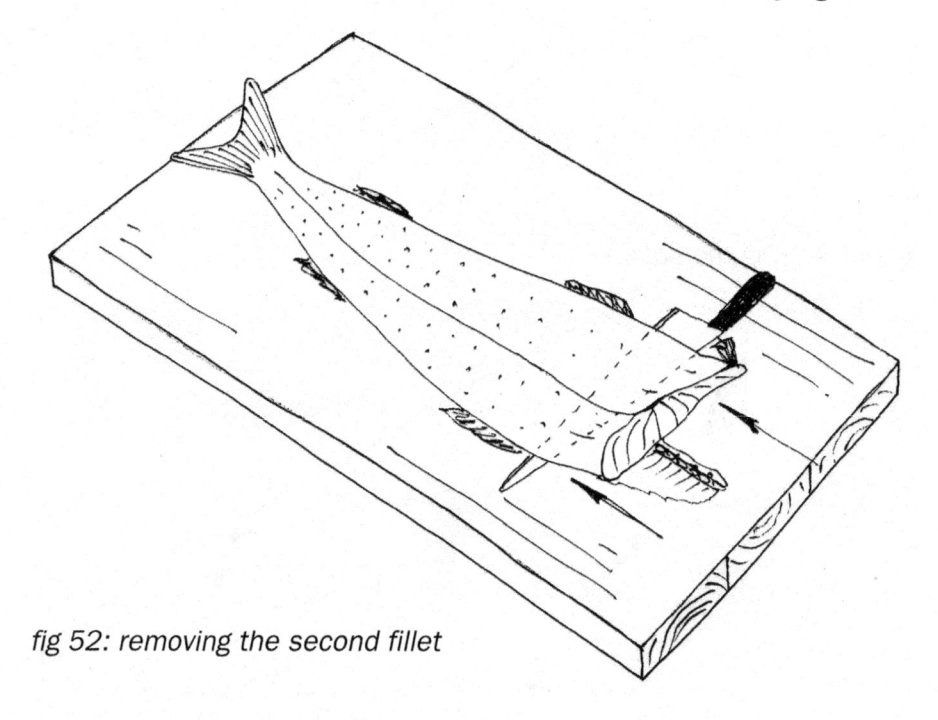

fig 52: removing the second fillet

The watchword here is take your time and be patient.

Turn both fillets flesh side up laying them flat on your cutting board. The rib bones can be removed at this point by cutting just beneath them removing a thin layer of flesh. This is easier said than done and requires quite a bit of patience. The rib bones can be left intact for smoking especially if you're not confident you can remove them without damaging the fillet.

fig 53: removing the ribs from the fillet

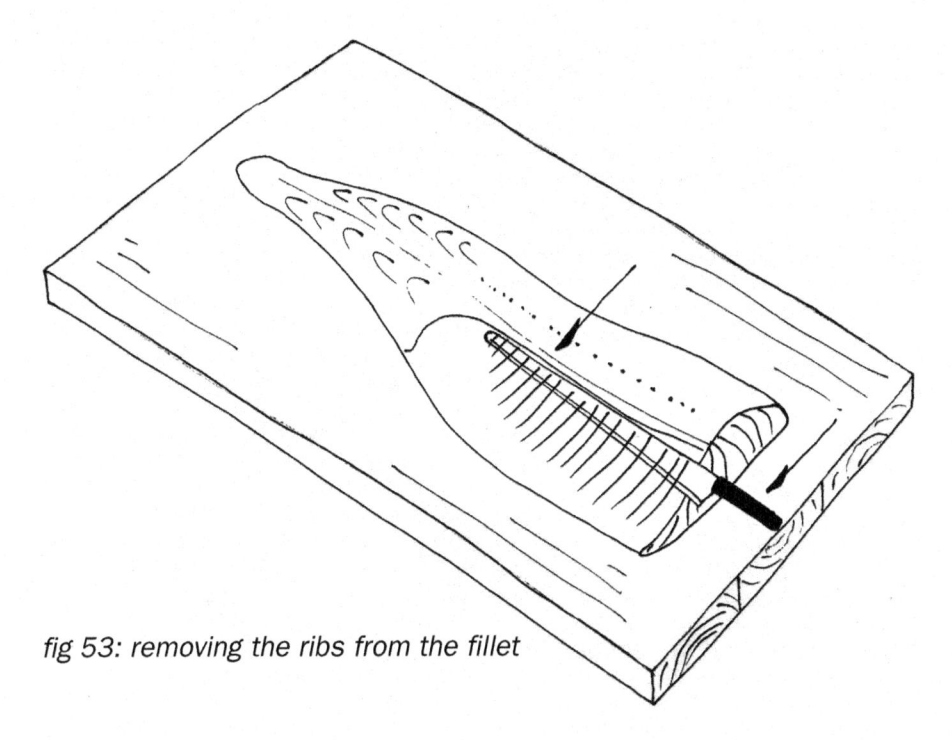

I prefer to remove them as it makes slicing the fillet much easier once it has been smoked; having said that there are some smokehouses that will cure the salmon with their rib bones intact removing them only after they have been cold smoked.

pin boning

Pin boning the fillet removes the lateral bones which run from the head to just below the vent. These are the small bones at right angles to the spine. They are not attached to the spine and are termed inter-muscular bones. There are several ways these can be removed, I prefer removing them before salting as the flesh is more pliable and soft and the bones can be removed causing less damage to the fillet. These bones can also be removed after salting. Some prefer this method as the flesh shrinks slightly after salting and the heads of the lateral bones are easier to find. The most effective method for locating the lateral bones is with your finger. Once found, using a pair of fish tweezers, gently tease the bone out of the fillet being careful not to damage the flesh. You'll be surprised at their length. This process takes a little time, and can be fiddly, but the finished fillet will be completely bone free and very easy to cut.

fig 54: pin boning the salmon fillet

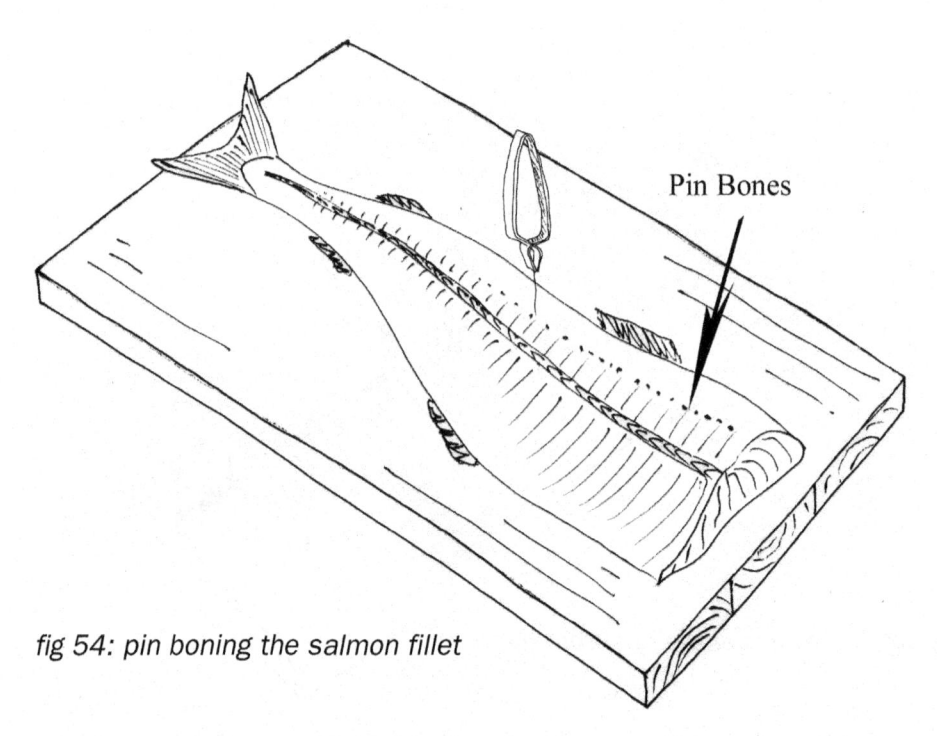

When you are happy all the bones are out of the salmon fillet, you can trim its edges to tidy up any scraggy ends or rough cuts removing any traces of fin or membrane, ensuring the gill plate or lug bone is intact. These bony plates will provide the fillet with structure and support for hanging in the smoker. At this point two small slits about 1cm in length should be made in the skin just behind the gill plate to facilitate threading the string you'll be using for hanging the fillets in the smoker.

If you prefer to lay the salmon on racks instead of suspending it it's not necessary to keep the gill plates intact when filleting and they can be discarded.

salt curing

The second step in making good smoked salmon is salting the fish. Salting was once the preservation step in the whole curing/smoking process. High levels of salt inhibited bacterial growth making the product safe to eat. With today's concern over high levels of salt in our diet and where lower levels of salt are preferred, one shouldn't rely solely on the salt as the primary preservative but should focus on using the freshest possible ingredients kept and handled at temperatures at or below 3°C.

Salting can be accomplished using either a strong solution of salt dissolved in water, known as brine, or dry salt sprinkled on the surface of the flesh. For most smoked salmon recipes dry salting is normal but brining can give a more uniform salting and is easier to prepare and use. The process of cold smoking salmon reduces the moisture content over time and this will need to be factored in if choosing to brine rather than dry salt. Please see the *basic cures and brines* chapter, page 25 for more detail.

For traditional smoked salmon, dry salting is the curing norm. This requires some experience before consistent results are obtained and is essential for cold smoking as it removes a higher percentage of moisture, rendering a drier, firmer product which takes the smoke better. One should seek to achieve somewhere between 10 to 15 per cent loss of weight from the original weight of the raw fish just through this initial salting. The dry salting method lowers the levels of moisture in the fillet through a process known as osmosis. This process leaches moisture from within the semi-permeable cell membrane of the fish in an attempt by the cell to equalise the salinity on both sides of the cell wall. Due to the extreme saltiness of the outer surface of the cell, this process of shedding moisture through the cell wall is a fruitless task as it will never achieve its goal. The process is handy for us because it also reduces the possibility of spoiling as bacteria require water to grow. There are a couple of other benefits worth mentioning here as after salt curing the texture of the fish becomes much firmer. This is useful when it comes to making those wonderfully thin translucent slices and it makes the salmon side much easier to handle too. One other benefit which is not so apparent is that by shedding the moisture you are effectively re-balancing the ratio of oils in the flesh to moisture content, giving you a slightly oily sheen when you slice the fish. This improves the texture and feel of the salmon and makes for a delightful eating experience.

dry salt cure

One can cure salmon with plain salt. Avoid salt containing any magnesium additives. Fine dry salt is perfect as is fine granular sea salt. Don't use products like Lo-Salt as this is packed with additives like potassium chloride. The addition of sugar to the cure can produce a sweet flavour in the salmon which is really nice. I also like to chop a little dill into the cure to add a nice herb flavour to the finished salmon but you do pretty much your own thing here and those of you keen on the curing process can derive a great deal of pleasure experimenting with different cure mixes. As a rule I tend to either use just plain salt for the purist approach or if I venture to use ingredients other than salt I tend to limit my additives to 25 per cent of the overall mix. Mix the salt and sugar in the ratio 3 to 1 (3 salt to 1 sugar) and add the chopped herbs to taste. It's fair to say that curing in itself is worth the contents of a whole book and there are no shortages of excellent reads on the book shelves and online so if you are interested it's worth a look.

OK, back to the preparation. Wash the fillet in cold water and pat dry with kitchen paper towel. Ensure you have a large enough non-metallic tray or dish for the fillet to lay completely flat. Non-metallic is important as you don't want the salt reacting with the tray or dish. Sprinkle some of the salt cure onto the base of the dish. Lay the fillet skin-side down on top of the salt cure. Apply a fine layer of salt so that it just covers the flesh. As you work towards the tail of the fillet reduce the salt in proportion to the thickness of the fillet so that at the tail of the fillet there is just a slight sprinkle of salt. When working towards the thicker part of the fillet slowly add more salt in direct proportion to the thickness of the fish. Repeat the process for the second fillet. The time required for salting varies depending on the size and thickness of the fillet and your own taste. Salt for too long and the fish will be unpalatable. Insufficient salting will result in your fillet spoiling through bacterial growth. Fattier fish like salmon and trout absorb salt reasonably slowly. White fish like haddock and cod on the other hand absorb salt very quickly and therefore should be timed accordingly. There is no hard and fast method for dry salting except a bit of trial and error. For an average-sized farmed salmon you are likely to buy, you should be looking to dry salt the sides for 4 to 6 hours.

After salting, wash the fillets in cold water to remove any remaining traces of salt and pat dry with kitchen towel. The fillets should be left to air dry for 12 to 24 hours before cold smoking or until a slightly shiny sticky salt coating has formed on the surface of the fillet. This is called the pellicle and is quite normal. The salting and air drying removes from 8 to10 per cent of the weight of the fillet (in water) leaving the flesh firm and springy to the touch. The pellicle is actually quite useful as the smoke likes to stick to a surface that it is miscible with.

brining

Brines can be prepared by dissolving salt in fresh water. Use only kosher salt, vacuum dried salt or flake salt for brines. These are pure salts. Avoid rock salt, sea salt and iodized salt because these contain impurities and additives that can cause bitterness and 'off' flavours. Curing salts should also be avoided since they contain nitrites (saltpetre). Commercially saltpetre is sometimes added to the cure to preserve the colour of the flesh in some meats. However, for home smoking it is difficult to get an even distribution of nitrite throughout the fish.

Any strength brine may be prepared (see page 28). The brine is made by dissolving 800gm of salt per 4.5 litres of water. Once the brine is made it should be chilled to 3°C or lower before use. This can be achieved by adding a handful of ice cubes to the water before adding the salt. The salt will melt the ice as it is added to the brine and in doing so the salt will change the ice from a solid to a liquid. For the scientists amongst us you'll know that in order to change the state of a substance you need energy which is derived from heat within the ice. Releasing this heat will reduce the temperature of the brine and compensate for the tepid water that you'll need to add to make up the volume.

The low temperature helps reduce bacterial growth and increases salt uptake into the fish. Place the fish in the brine for 20 minutes to 3 hours depending on the desired taste. Weaker brines (using less than 800gm of salt per 4.5 litres) can be used with a correspondingly longer soaking time.

Fish should be thoroughly rinsed in cold water to remove excess brine if it has been kept in brine for long periods of time (one hour or more). Brining usually takes only a short while for salmon (around 15 minutes). For a lightly salted product (brining times less that 1 hour), a fresh water rinse is sufficient to remove excess brine. Before hot smoking, remove excess moisture from the fish by patting dry with paper towel.

To ensure you have sufficient quantities of brine to cure your meat or fish it is important to match the quantity of brine to the weight of meat or fish. The brine-to-meat/fish ratio should be about 3 to 1. That basically means 3 parts brine to 1 part fish (by weight). For example, 4.5kg of fish will require 13.5kg of brine (approximately 18 litres; 4.5 litres of brine weighs about 3.6kg).

drying

Once the fish has been brined, it is usually dried before smoking. Drying accomplishes two things. It allows the salt to penetrate and to become evenly distributed throughout the flesh. This may require anywhere from 2 to 24 hours depending on its thickness (6 to 8 hours for a 2.5cm thick piece). Secondly, the surface of the fish dries to form a 'pellicle' or shiny slightly sticky coat. The pellicle seals in moisture and makes the appearance of the finished product much better.

Drying should take place in the fridge after curing and before smoking. For salmon the fillet should be placed in the refrigerator while drying to avoid bacterial growth. One consequence of the drying process is to allow the salt to equalise throughout the fish and of course for the pellicle to form. During the drying phase, try to keep temperatures below 3°C.

Forming a pellicle sometimes requires warmer temperatures and can be achieved during the initial stages of smoking. It may take upwards of 30 minutes to 3 hours to form a good pellicle. This is largely dependent on the smoker temperature and relative humidity. If possible, avoid longer times at ambient temperatures because the potential for bacterial growth increases. It may be worth keeping the salmon in the fridge to dry when faced with high ambient temperatures. Part of the cold smoking process is to further reduce the weight of the fish while the smoke is being applied. This continued drying will further prevent bacterial growth. The finished product can achieve as much as a 25 per cent reduction in weight from the initial raw salmon weight.

smoking

The fourth step of the process is smoking. There are many recipes for smoking using different times and temperatures and woods, but in terms of smoking there are only two basic methods:

hot smoking: where the internal product temperature reaches 82°C and higher resulting in a cooked, smoked product such as Arbroath Smokies and bloaters.

cold smoking: where the internal product temperature is kept below 30°C. The resulting product is essentially raw, cured smoked fish such as lox or Scottish style salmon.

For most people who want instant results, hot smoking is the most popular form and easiest to produce in stovetop smokers and dedicated hot smokers like the Bradley smoker. Hot smoking has gained popularity worldwide as it closely follows many of the principles of barbequing. However, as the aim of cold smoking was initially to preserve food it fits more closely with the values of low-impact living and therefore it's my preferred method.

The temperatures recommended for hot smoking are high enough to kill most bacteria. Cold smoke temperatures are not hot enough to kill bacteria and that's why it is important to work hygienically with fresh ingredients at low temperatures.

hot smoking

Cook the fish to 82°C internal temperature (use a thermometer or temperature probe, see page 179 for details) for at least 30 minutes at some time during smoking, preferably toward the end. This temperature will kill most bacteria and combined with refrigeration will ensure a safe product. Typically, hot smoking should bring the internal temperature of the product to 82°C within 15 to 20 minutes after placing it in the smoker. The actual time it takes will largely depend on the size of the fish or meat. Use a standard meat thermometer to monitor internal temperature. Insert the thermometer into the thickest part of the fish.

Depending on the desired finished product, hot smoking should take anywhere from 10 to 30 minutes. Shorter cooking times will generally preserve the moisture in the finished product.

cold smoking

If cold smoked fish will not be cooked prior to eating, it is essential to freeze the fish for the correct time and at the correct temperature to destroy any parasites that may be present in the uncooked fish, see page 129 for further details. If you are purchasing your fish from a store it is highly unlikely the fish has not already been through this step.

- temperature control is critical. Never allow the internal product temperature to exceed 30°C – this is because at 35°C the fish will start to cook.

- it is difficult to cold smoke in areas of high humidity. If relative humidity cannot be reduced below 75 per cent at air temperatures under 30°C then cold smoking is difficult to do.
- depending on the desired finished product, smoking can take anywhere from 2 hours to 7 days.

product storage

The final and most important step in producing smoked fish is product storage. Most smoked products have usually been subjected to brining or salting prior to smoking. Where low levels of salt are preferred it must be considered that the fish is essentially a fresh product. There is not enough salt, smoke or heat employed to preserve the product. The potential for bacterial spoilage and botulism exists.

After the fish has been smoked, allow it to cool to room temperature (this will prevent condensation) and then do one of the following:

1. Wrap and refrigerate below 3°C until consumed. Use a good plastic wrap and/or aluminium foil. Lightly salted and smoked product can last as long as 5 to 7 days in the refrigerator. Ensure your refrigerator maintains a consistent temperature.

2. Wrap and freeze. Use a good freezer wrap and aluminium foil to protect the product. Properly protected smoked salmon will last for 2 to 3 months in tip top condition. Any longer than that in the freezer and the salmon will start to show signs of 'freezer burn' and this will show in the defrosted fish.

3. Another popular method for storing smoked fish is sealing the products in vacuum packages. Home vacuum packing makes it easy to protect smoked fish. BUT, vacuum packaged smoked fish MUST be kept under refrigerated or frozen storage.

slicing your very own smoked salmon

A popular method of slicing smoked salmon from a whole side is to work from the gill end or thick end of the fillet slicing at an angle towards the gills and working back towards the tail end with every slice. At first this can be quite difficult to do and it takes a little practice to master the technique. Try an angle of around 60 degrees from the vertical to start with and as you get more skilled at it you can increase the angle to make the slices longer. Try and keep the slices around 2mm to 3mm thick, any thinner and the salmon flakes may start to fall apart.

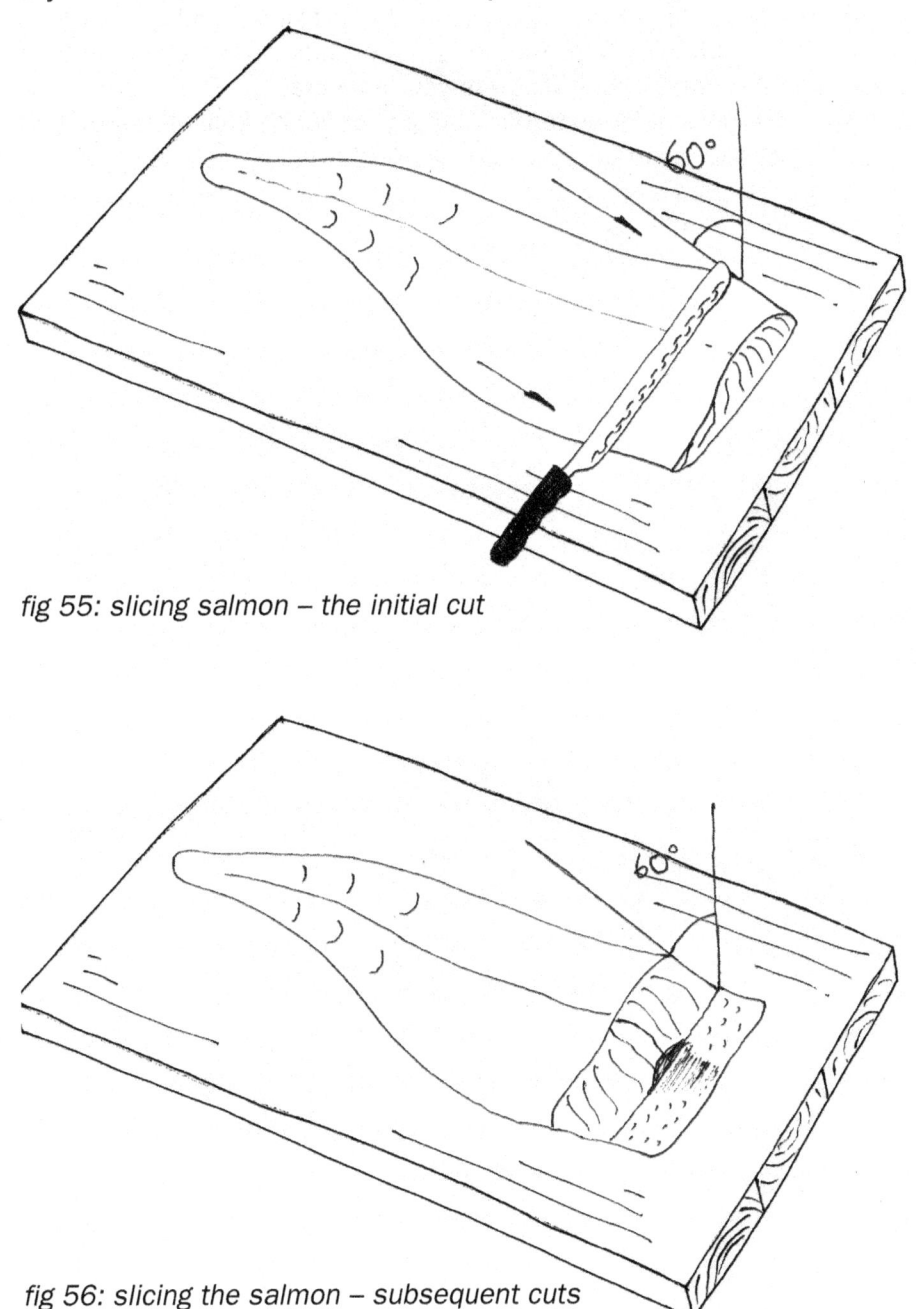

fig 55: slicing salmon – the initial cut

fig 56: slicing the salmon – subsequent cuts

The watchword here is 'take your time'.

All in all making your own smoked salmon is something that can be achieved with a little effort. The method I use to teach others is pretty basic. I will emphasise here that in terms of adding ingredients to your curing salt the only limiting factor is your imagination. The internet is a really good source of ideas for flavouring your curing salt. Herbs that go well with fish like dill or tarragon are excellent to add that little extra. The addition of sugars and spices to the mix make the permutations of flavours almost limitless.

smoking meat

Smoking meat is a real passion of mine. There is nothing quite like your own smoked bacon and it's something I've enjoyed for a good few years now. I was first introduced to smoking meat some time after my smoked salmon exploits and after I had learned the art of salt curing my own bacon and other cured meats. Curing meat or *charcuterie* as it's more popularly known should be the subject of a book in itself as it is one of the most rewarding forms of food alchemy I've come across. The magic salt works with fish and meat is a wonder to behold and is something that once it's captivated you, will never leave you. This is the thing with curing and smoking meats you see, there are so many cuts of meat, so many different styles of curing, countless varieties of herbs and spices and lots of different woods to smoke that a chapter will barely do the subject justice.

Before meat is cold smoked it will usually have undergone some form of curing or salting process in a similar way to fish in order to reduce its moisture content and improve its texture and flavour. To that end the addition of smoke further improves the texture by allowing the meat to continue to dry whilst receiving smoke. Cold smoke works really well allowing one to produce delicately textured, cured meat treats with the most amazing depth of flavour. What more needs to be said?

Well, I said just one chapter wouldn't do justice to the subject but here goes. I would prefer you to see this as an introduction to meat smoking as opposed to something more akin to a chapter on meat curing and I know that the vast majority of people like to take advantage of a barbeque to add a wonderful smoky flavour to their meat. After all this is one of the easiest and most accessible ways to smoke meat and is certainly one of the most popular ways of smoking food I know. That said I will look at both cold and hot smoking methods in this chapter and include some ideas for adding smoke to your barbequed meat.

There are a few terms in this chapter may not be familiar to you. I use the term 'blue' to refer to red meat that is essentially still raw. It is often used to describe red meat that has been cooked on the outside and remains uncooked in the middle. The wrong side of rare one might say. The other term I use is 'pellicle'. The pellicle is a film on the surface of whatever you are going to smoke. It takes the form of a slightly sticky glaze which is clearly visible on the surface and is particularly useful for the smoke to adhere to.

smoked beef fillet

Beef fillet can be hot or cold smoked. If you are hot smoking beef fillet it should be brined for about twenty minutes in an 80 per cent brine solution. I find that pan frying the beef fillet before smoking not only improves its finished look but also develops the flavours in the meat to complement the smoke. I prefer to pan fry until the fillet is still raw in the middle (blue) so that when it goes into the hot smoker, the heat and smoke will continue the cooking process until the fillet is rare to medium. Any more than this and the fillet would have lost its charm. From the pan I transfer the fillet to the hot smoker and hot smoke with oak, hickory or mesquite for about 12 minutes for a 200g fillet. If you choose to hot smoke directly from the brine you'll find the meat will come out of the smoker with some colour from the smoke but otherwise it will look a little pale. It will still taste delicious but will lack flavour complexity from the caramelisation of the natural meat juices. If you are using a dedicated hot smoker with temperature control you can cook it low and slow keeping the temperature at around 75°C to 80°C. The beef will be done when the internal temperature has reached 71°C. This may take a little while longer for a 200g fillet than the 12 minutes mentioned earlier.

If you're cold smoking beef fillet I'll assume you're using a piece of fillet about 500g. Feel free to scale the ingredients in proportion to the size of the meat you're preparing. You'll need enough cure to coat the outside of the meat sufficiently if you're using a larger cut.

50g salt
10g dark brown sugar
½ teaspoon black pepper
½ teaspoon fresh or dried thyme

500g beef fillet

Mix all the ingredients for the cure together in a bowl and rub well into the fillet. Place the fillet and the cure in a sealed plastic container or plastic zip bag and place in the fridge. Turn after 12 hours and remove from the fridge after 24 hours. Rinse under cold running water, pat dry with paper towel and return it to the fridge for another 24 hours to dry out. By this time the beef will have lost around 12 to 15 per cent of its raw weight and formed a pellicle and will be ready to smoke. Cold smoke the beef fillet for between 12 and 24 hours, checking that your beef has lost 25 per cent of its raw weight by the end. The weight loss is important as is the salting as it renders the meat safe to eat without cooking. Rest the meat for a day in the fridge and then slice thinly. Serve with a green salad and shards of parmesan (you can even try smoked parmesan) with rocket and balsamic vinegar. You can apply a similar method to duck breast adding a few crushed juniper berries and thyme to the cure mix.

hot smoked chicken

Chicken breasts can be either hot or cold smoked. To hot smoke I pan fry the breasts off the bone to caramelise the outside taking care not to cook them through fully; they can benefit from a light brining before pan frying. I then finish them off in the stovetop smoker for about 10 minutes just to give them a light smoking and to complete the cooking process without overdoing and drying them out. Chicken can be hot smoked with your favourite wood in a dedicated hot smoker like a Bradley smoker for two to three hours at around 90°C. Hickory works well with chicken as do the fruit woods like cherry and apple.

Nowadays many home barbeques come complete with lids and this make smoking food easily accessible to everyone. If you are hot smoking the chicken on a barbeque this method can work for all cuts but you will have to be a little careful not to overcook the breasts and dry them out or worse still cause a flare-up from too much fat on the legs and thighs. If you have a lid for your barbeque this is very easy. Just cook the chicken until it's about two thirds done, add some pre-soaked wood chips of your choice (apple, hickory, oak, sweet chestnut or beech all go well with chicken) and finish off the cooking with the lid down.

Fear not, if you don't have a lid on your barbeque place a sheet of foil big enough to cover the chicken turning down the edges to form a cap over your cooking. If you don't have any foil it is possible to use an upturned roasting tray, this will trap the smoke and do the same job as a lid. For both methods, keep an eye on what you are doing just in case of a flare-up.

It is also possible to use a perforated metal container or a cast iron pot to hold your chips. This has two benefits. Firstly it cuts down on the likelihood of a flare-up with wood directly on hot coals and secondly, when you've finished the chicken you can remove the container from the coal saving the remaining unburnt chips for your next batch.

If you would like to cold smoke chicken it's possible to either add smoke to a cooked chicken breast, and this works well, or completely cure the chicken beforehand, drying it in the fridge and smoking it in the cold smoker for up to eight hours. Just keep an eye on the temperature or your chicken will dry out and become unpalatable.

smoked duck

Duck and smoke were made for each other: follow the recipe given for beef fillet, page 146, to achieve the cold smoked duck 'ham' which, when sliced thinly, is a sheer delight with a light green salad.

The method used for hot smoking duck is very similar to chicken and can deliver wonderful results. Brine the duck breast in an 80 per cent brine for 10 to 15 minutes, see the *basic cures and brines* chapter page 25. Rinse the meat and pat dry with paper kitchen towel. To achieve a nice colour on the duck breast I like to pan fry the breast so it is partially cooked. This caramelises the skin of the breast developing flavour and colour. Place the duck breast in a small stovetop smoker using about a teaspoon of dust and hot smoke for about ten minutes to impart the smoky flavour to the duck and complete the cooking.

There is another method for hot smoking a duck breast but it is quite longwinded requiring changes in temperature over time. Essentially it is a longer hot smoking process which maintains the redness of the duck flesh on the inside by utilising quite low temperatures in the initial hot smoking phase finishing off with a warmer cooking and smoking phase at the end of the process. The latter method is typically how commercial smoke houses produce hot smoked products (fish and meat) but is likely to be outside the scope of most budding amateurs. The technique of finishing the hot smoking using elevated temperatures is to improve the look of the finished product by liberating some of the oils from within the fish or meat.

smoked venison

Venison can be both hot and cold smoked. It can be hot smoked in much the same way as in the beef fillet recipe, page 146, but please consider, as venison is a lean meat, it may be necessary when pan frying to add a little oil to make up for the lack of fat on the muscle.

The most popular parts of venison are either leg or shoulder steaks and these can both be treated in a similar way. Venison tenderloin is a very nice cut of meat if not a little pricy but if you can obtain it you can treat it with just a little more finesse as it is, as its name suggests, tender. Brine the tenderloin for 10 to 15 minutes in an 80 per cent brine. Pat dry with paper towel and pan fry lightly to give the venison some colour and caramelisation. Transfer to the smoker and smoke with oak, apple or cherry for a further 10 to 15 minutes until the venison is still rare in the middle.

To cold smoke venison first soak the venison in an 80 per cent brine for four hours ensuring it is totally submerged. Rinse and pat dry and allow it to rest in the fridge for 12 hours or until the formation of the pellicle. Then cold smoke the venison for six to eight hours using a mild wood like beech or one of the fruit woods. The venison can now be loosely wrapped in muslin and air dried for five to seven days. This is best done in a temperature-controlled environment not exceeding 15°C. The venison can now be cut very thinly and served in a similar manner to that of *prosciutto* ham or any other cured ham for that matter. It's important that the finished venison has lost approximately 25 per cent of its raw weight; the loss of moisture during the salt curing and cold smoking process works towards making the venison safe to eat. Temperature is of course important too and one must ensure that this is managed throughout the process.

smoked lamb

Lamb can be prepared and smoked in a similar way to venison. One key point to remember is that lamb is much fattier than venison so when hot smoking there is little need when initially browning the meat (see previous section) to add any fat as you'll find there is sufficient.

When it comes to smoking lamb I think that the choice of smoke is important. Lamb has a very distinctive flavour and this will be heightened by the initial brining process. Lamb can take a strong smoke and I have had great success using hickory or oak to add flavour. Interestingly, the use of herbs can be employed here and I have used dried rosemary as a smoking wood for the last hour of cold smoking to add a familiar and complementing flavour and aroma to the finished lamb. Equally when hot smoking lamb the use of a small quantity of rosemary sprigs mixed in with your choice of wood chip will achieve a similar end result.

If you air dry lamb, in much the same way as air dried ham or for that matter air dried duck, exposing fine slices of the lamb for a few minutes to cold smoke from rosemary dust will add a delicate aromatic quality to the slices elevating them to mythical status (in my opinion). This is a tactic one can also use when serving *prosciutto* or Parma ham but instead of a herb smoke I would recommend the use of a fruit wood like apple, cherry, or if you prefer, perhaps oak for the more traditional amongst you.

pastrami

Pastrami is a cured, smoked beef brisket or 'flat' as it is known. It enjoys huge popularity in the US and growing popularity over here in Europe. Pastrami is cured with seasonings and hot smoked with more seasonings. The main flavours associated with pastrami are pepper, coriander, garlic and paprika. I have made pastrami using a 2.3kg brisket which is a manageable size and therefore this recipe is based on a brisket that size. If you cannot find a brisket that size then adjust the recipe accordingly.

    2.3kg cut of beef brisket

to cure the brisket
    50g salt
    20g sugar (optional)
    5.75g Prague powder #1 (used at the rate of 2.5g per kilogram of meat)
    2 tablespoons black peppercorns, crushed
    2 tablespoons ground coriander
    2 teaspoons garlic powder
    2 teaspoons paprika
    a sealable plastic bag zip lock bag or similar; a vacuum sealer bag would be fine

to season the brisket before hot smoking
- 2 tablespoons black peppercorns, crushed
- 2 tablespoons ground coriander
- 2 teaspoons garlic powder
- 2 teaspoons paprika

Trim any excess fat, skin and sinew from your brisket and pat dry with paper towel. With the brisket on a chopping board use a small knife to pierce both the upper and lower surfaces of the meat at about one inch, 25mm, intervals. This will allow the cure to do its thing evenly through the whole brisket. Place the brisket in a non-metallic dish.

Mix all the ingredients for the cure together and spread it evenly over both sides of the brisket, rubbing it thoroughly into the surface of the meat. Transfer the brisket into a sealed vacuum bag or other sealable bag. When doing this try to remove as much air as possible from the bag and ensure that the bag doesn't leak during the curing stage. If there is a chance the bag may leak then ensure you place the bag on a tray or shallow dish to catch any liquid that mey be produced during the curing process. Allow the brisket to cure in the fridge for seven days turning over daily.

After the curing stage is complete, remove the brisket from the fridge and discard the bag. Rinse the brisket under cold running water to remove all traces of the cure. Soak in sufficient cold water to submerge the brisket for one hour, drain and pat dry with kitchen towel. Lay the brisket in a non-metallic tray. Mix all the ingredients for the seasoning together. Apply the seasoning to the brisket in the ratio of one third on the bottom and sides with the remaining two thirds on the top surface. The point of this is to give the brisket a herb and spice crust as it cooks through.

The next stage of the process is the most important part in terms of achieving the right texture. It is really important not to overcook the brisket otherwise it will become tough and dry. Low and slow is the key here, low temperatures and a long cooking time will ensure you get the right texture. Brisket can be a little tough if it is not cooked for long enough or if it's cooked at too high a temperature. The curing process starts to break this toughness down and this continues with the cooking and smoking process too providing the temperature is maintained at the correct level.

hot smoke method

Plan to hot smoke your brisket for around four hours at 80°C aiming for an internal temperature of 72°C. The internal temperature can be checked using a food probe. Smoke with oak or a fruit wood like cherry or apple to impart a wonderfully aromatic smoky flavour and colour to your pastrami.

cold smoke method

If you haven't got a hot smoker you can cook your brisket in the oven before smoking it. Be careful here as even gas mark 1 (140°C) will be too hot. Some electric ovens allow temperatures as low as 50°C so you will need a little experimentation to get this part exactly right. You are aiming for an internal temperature of 72°C in the thickest part of the brisket. Once this temperature has been achieved for 20 minutes, remove from the oven and allow to cool.

To achieve this internal temperature you will need to aim for an oven temperature slightly higher than your target internal temperature as there will be a lag in temperature rise for the internal part of the meat. This may sound obvious but it's worth mentioning because in order to achieve the internal temperature and prevent overcooking the brisket on the outside it is absolutely imperative to take your time cooking this slab of meat so the outside temperature doesn't exceed 80°C. It takes a long time for the inside of the meat to reach temperature hence the long cooking time. Have patience, once the brisket has cooled it can be placed in a cold smoker for between two and four hours (depending on your preferred taste).

spicy smoked beef jerky

This is such a simple recipe and method I'm surprised more people don't try this at home for themselves. Well here's hoping I can help to change that perception a little. First of all you'll need to get hold of a topside or sirloin joint weighing about 1.8kg. Unwrap it and pat it dry using paper towel. The drier the meat is the easier it will be to slice thinly as it won't be flopping about all over the board. If it's too wet then allow it to dry on an open plate in the fridge for about eight hours. Trim off all the sinew and fat. Sirloin or topside joints can have some thickness to them so next, using an extremely sharp knife, slice the joint in half horizontally so it's about a 25mm thick slab. Slice thinly (2mm).

Make up your marinade as follows:

- ½ cup light soya sauce
- ½ cup Worcestershire sauce
- 1 teaspoon garlic powder
- (You can substitute a crushed clove of garlic but as the smoked beef is essentially raw the garlic will remain raw; you could use a roasted clove or two)
- 1 teaspoon chilli powder
- 1 teaspoon ground black pepper
- 2 tablespoons sugar or honey
- ½ an onion

Take the onion and chop it finely by hand or in a food processor. Place all the ingredients into a plastic container and mix them together well. Add your strips of beef and allow them to marinade for 12 hours. To turn them into beef jerky you'll need to dry them out. One of the best ways to achieve this without going to the expense of buying a dedicated food dehydrator is to use a fan oven on its lowest setting. Arrange the marinated strips of beef on wire racks to dry in the oven at no more than 50°C. If you are in any doubt check the temperature with a probe before attempting this stage. I find once you have the oven working at its lowest temperature the door of the oven can be left ajar to allow excess moisture to escape and this assists greatly in the drying process.

When the beef feels firm but pliable remove the food racks from the oven to allow the jerky to cool to room temperature. The strips of jerky are now ready to go in the smoker to receive some cold smoke for around four hours. The seasoning used in this recipe is quite strong and therefore it is necessary to use a smoke that packs a similar punch and can stand shoulder to shoulder with the strong flavours in the marinade. Cold smoking for four hours is sufficient but as I've mentioned before it is a matter of personal choice and the jerky can be smoked to suit your own taste. This jerky recipe yields around 1kg of the best beef jerky you have ever had. You will never have to pay ridiculously expensive prices for 50g ever again.

Beef jerky can be stored in the fridge in sealed containers for a couple of weeks. If you choose to vacuum pack it and freeze it you'll get over a year from it.

In terms of added value, providing the ratio between your raw ingredients and shop bought jerky keep pace, using my method you would typically yield 'a product with a value some six times more than the raw ingredients. That's not a bad days work by anyone's standards. Beef jerky makes the ideal trail food and this method of preserving meat has been employed for millennia especially in countries with the weather to dry meat in the open sun.

smoked salt

Smoked salt has in recent years become a bit of a phenomenon in the gourmet world. The use of smoke purely as a flavour in salt is a great way of introducing smoke to all kinds of food in the form of a seasoning. It's somewhat ironic that smoke was used as a preservative as was salt and here they are together taking seasoning flavourings to another dimension.

Smoking salt yourself can on the face of it is a straightforward affair and under the right circumstances it can be. There are, however, a couple of things you need to keep an eye out for when smoking salt. Although not strictly hygroscopic by definition, salt will absorb moisture if there is any available to absorb. While this may not be a problem when smoking for a short period of time, when the smoking period is extended the moisture produced with the smoke can cause your salt to become wet, returning it to brine. Not in itself a problem but unless you want to spend hours drying out your salt in a low oven there are alternative methods you can adopt of to avoid the problem in the first place.

moisture

The moisture produced alongside smoke when wood burns is a natural part of the chemistry of combustion. There is just no real way of producing smoke from wood without this inevitable by-product. So, in an attempt to control it there are a few tricks that can be employed to assist in removing the unwanted moisture from the smoke. I find that whenever I smoke salt in my cardboard smoker I rarely if ever suffer the indignity of removing wet salt from it. Somehow inside the smoker the cardboard acts as a sponge tending to absorb the moisture in the smoke. The temperature of the smoke also plays a part in the moisture game as the cooler the smoke gets the more chance it will condense out on the surfaces within the smoker including the salt.

cardboard

The cardboard smoker, initially dry has a similar ability to absorb moisture as salt, I haven't done the science but experience tells me this is so. Anyone with an all metal smokehouse will tell you how much smoke condensate runs down the walls and drips from the ceiling. Although I have not had the opportunity to experiment extensively with this finding, any salt smokers out there experiencing problems with additional moisture could try adding a few discreetly hung sheets of cardboard in the smoker as a moisture regulator.

appendix a: nitrite concentration in dry cure mixes

PPM	1	2	4	10	15	20	30	40	50	60	70	80
100	1.60	3.20	6.40	16.00	24.00	32.00	48.00	64.00	80.00	96.00	112.00	128.00
110	1.76	3.52	7.04	17.60	26.40	35.20	52.80	70.40	88.00	105.60	123.20	140.80
120	1.92	3.84	7.68	19.20	28.80	38.40	57.60	76.80	96.00	115.20	134.40	153.60
130	2.08	4.16	8.32	20.80	31.20	41.60	62.40	83.20	104.00	124.80	145.60	166.40
140	2.24	4.48	8.96	22.40	33.60	44.80	67.20	89.60	112.00	134.40	156.80	179.20
150	2.40	4.80	9.60	24.00	36.00	48.00	72.00	96.00	120.00	144.00	168.00	192.00
160	2.56	5.12	10.24	25.60	38.40	51.20	76.80	102.40	128.00	153.60	179.20	204.80
170	2.72	5.44	10.88	27.20	40.80	54.40	81.60	108.80	136.00	163.20	190.40	217.60
180	2.88	5.76	11.52	28.80	43.20	57.60	86.40	115.20	144.00	172.80	201.60	230.40
190	3.04	6.08	12.16	30.40	45.60	60.80	91.20	121.60	152.00	182.40	212.80	243.20
200	3.20	6.40	12.80	32.00	48.00	64.00	96.00	128.00	160.00	192.00	224.00	256.00
210	3.36	6.72	13.44	33.60	50.40	67.20	100.80	134.40	168.00	201.60	235.20	268.80
220	3.52	7.04	14.08	35.20	52.80	70.40	105.60	140.80	176.00	211.20	246.40	281.60

Quantity of Meat (Kg) to be cured Prague Powder #1 - Cure #1

Table 01 Prague Powder #1 Cure #1. Weight in gms. For a given quantity of meat.

appendix b: brining tables

Percentage Salt in Solution	Percentage Salt by Wgt.	Grams of Salt per L water	Grams of Salt per Imp gal. water	Pounds of Salt per Imp gal. water
10	2.640	27	123	4oz
20	5.279	55	250	8.8oz
30	7.919	86	391	13.8oz
40	10.558	118	537	1lb-3oz
50	13.198	152	692	1lb-8oz
55	14.517	170	774	1lb-11oz
60	15.837	188	855	1lb-14oz
70	18.477	226	1028	2lb-4oz
80	21.116	267	1215	2lb-11oz
90	23.755	311	1415	3lb-2oz
100	26.395	358	1629	3lb-9oz

appendix c: brine recipes

spicy brine

4.5 litres at 40 per cent SAL

4.5 litres cold water
526g salt
5 bay leaves, crushed
6 teaspoons pepper
4 tablespoons mace
8 teaspoons allspice
1 tablespoon cloves
2 tablespoons juniper berries, crushed

Combine all the ingredients together in a spice grinder and blend into a fine powder. Add this to the brine solution and bring it to the boil. Remove the brine from the heat and allow it to cool. When it reaches room temperature chill it in the fridge until it is about 4°C. Add your fish or meat and allow it to brine for four to six hours.

spiced honey brine

1 litre at 40 per cent SAL to make a hot smoked honey salmon fillet

1 litre cold water
120g salt
10 cloves
10 allspice berries
1 bay leaf
200g honey
5 tablespoons dark rum
juice and zest of 1 lemon

750g salmon fillet (with the skin on)

Combine the cloves, all spice and bay leaves and grind in a spice grinder until finely ground. If you have ground all spice then omit this from the grinder. Add the spice mix, honey, rum, lemon juice and zest to the brine, bring to the boil and allow it to cool before chilling in the fridge.

Place the salmon fillet, skin side up, in a non-metallic dish and cover with the brine. Place it in the refrigerator. Allow the fish to cure for about 2 hours then rinse the fillet in fresh, cold running water and dry with paper kitchen towel. Place the salmon on a drying rack in the fridge and allow to air dry for a further two hours then hot smoke the salmon for about one and a half hours, ensuring the temperature remains at around 71°C. This will ensure the fish will retain most of its moisture as it cooks.

soy sauce and wine brine

1 litre at slightly over 40 per cent SAL
300ml cold water
400ml soy sauce
300ml dry white wine
120g salt
150g sugar
½ teaspoon onion powder*
½ teaspoon garlic powder
½ teaspoon pepper
½ teaspoon Tabasco sauce

750g salmon fillet (with the skin on)

Mix the dry ingredients together and grind to a fine dust using a spice grinder. Make up the brine from the salt, water, soy sauce and wine. Mix in the dry ingredients ensuring they combine well with the brine. Place the salmon, skin side down, in a non-metallic dish and cover with the brine. Leave to cure in the refrigerator for 6 to 8 hours, keeping all of the fish covered with brine. The brine will be slightly stronger than 40% as the Soy sauce contains salt and depending on which variety you choose it will be a little stronger than 40% but not too much as to be of any concern.

Hot smoking times will depend on the thickness of the fish and the type of smoker you are using. Aim to hot smoke the salmon until it is just done – it will be between 20 and 30 minutes for a 750g fillet. Enjoy!

*If you can't get hold of onion powder you can use half a finely sliced small onion instead.

appendix d: summary of differences between smoking methods

Description	Cold Smoking	Hot Smoking
Brine Cure	Yes – with the obvious exception of products like cheese and nuts. Used to assist the process of preservation	Not necessarily as a preserving agent but used widely as a flavour enhancement.
Time duration	Measured in hours and sometimes days for a really smokey flavour in some food like bacon and hams.	Rarely more than a couple of hours and often less than an hour as part of a cooking process. Usually limited by the cooking time.
Temperature	Below 30°C as an absolute maximum and often at much lower temperatures. Not below 0°C as smoke will not penetrate the flesh.	Above 75°C and up to 100°C as part of the cooking process. Can achieve much higher temperatures on a barbeque or above open flames.
Finished product	Essentially a raw product, and apart from Smoked Salmon, cheese or nuts may require further cooking.	Will produce a cooked product and would be ready to eat directly from the smoker or when cool.
Dust or chips	Largely depends on the method of generating smoke. If the smoke is generated in the same compartment as the food, where temp is critical, dust would be preferable for a cooler smoke and slower heat production.	Chips are preferable for hot smoking as they will combust easily generating lots of good smoke. Chips will last longer than dust under the same circumstances producing smoke for longer. Chips are better on a BBQ for the same reason and will flame less readily than dust.
Typical products	Kippers, Cold Smoked Salmon or Trout, Smoked Bacon, Smoked cheese and nuts.	Hot smoked mackerel, Arbroath Smokies, Smoked sausage

appendix e: dos and don'ts when sourcing and processing wood

Do ensure.	How?
You remove all traces of chain oil from the wood you use.	By using a planer or saw on the ends of the wood to remove oil that has contaminated the wood
You use wood that is not diseased	By ensuring the bark is in good condition and there is no obvious growth or infestation on or in the wood
Your wood shaving or dust source is not contaminated.	Only purchase food grade chippings or dust or source from a reliable supplier you can trust.
You use appropriate PPE when making shavings and chippings with power tools	By wearing hearing and eye protection. In addition to this, gloves are a must when using a chipper
Don't	**Why?**
Use soft woods or anything that contains pine or spruce	Because these woods contain large amounts of resin and can impart a bitter tastes to food.
Use bark from trees with a thick bark like Oak or Sweet Chestnut	Because this bark can trap dirt, disease, bugs and fungal spores all of which can spoil your dust or chips.
Seal your wood shavings or chippings until they have dried sufficiently.	Because any trapped moisture will cause the contents to decompose into compost.
Don't inhale wood dust particles when you manufacture your own shavings or chippings	Because they are hazardous to your respiratory health. Always use the appropriate PPE a suitable facemask will be sufficient for short durations.
Don't use woods from poisonous trees and plants	It's possible that some of the compounds in poisonous woods may be transmitted to your food. The rule of thumb is to only smoke with woods that produce an edible crop or are widely known to be safe. If in doubt don't use it.

appendix f:
burning characteristics

Wood Particle Size	Combustion characteristics
Fine Dust (< 1mm)	Has a tendency to smoulder slowly when the conditions are right. Likely to be affected by moisture and less likely to initiate flaming combustion unless there is substantial airflow influencing the area of combustion. Dry material can smoulder predictably with little chance of a flare-up little chance of self-extinguishing if the conditions and moisture content are right.
Coarse Dust (1mm-2mm)	Has less of a tendency to smoulder freely without a slight airflow in the area of combustion. Likely to be affected by moisture and is less likely to initiate flaming combustion. Dry material can smoulder under the right conditions but is more likely to self-extinguish with insufficient airflow.
Fine Chips (2mm-5mm)	Have a tendency to smoulder when there is sufficient airflow. Moderate likelihood they will be affected by moisture. Moderate likelihood they will flare up with sufficient airflow. Will tend to self-extinguish in still conditions.
Coarse Chips (5-10mm)	Have a tendency to self-extinguish if left to smoulder in still conditions. More Likely to sustain a flame on lighting if dry. Likely to be moderately affected by moisture content. Can sustain a smoulder with sufficient airflow.
Small Chunks (10mm–25mm)	Have a tendency burn on lighting especially if dry. Moderately affected by moisture content. Less likely to smoulder unless supported by sufficient airflow. Likely to self-extinguish if left in still conditions
Large Chunks (25mm-100mm)	Take time to ignite and burn. Large chunks have a tendency to burn well when stacked with air around the chunks. Will smoulder providing there is sufficient airflow through the wood chunks.
Disks or logs (>100mm)	Take a longer time to ignite then chunks and once combusting can smoulder providing there is sufficient airflow. Will burn freely if stacked with sufficient air around discs.
Shavings (5mm-15mm)	Thin shavings have a tendency to ignite and flare up with flaming combustion if the airflow surrounding them is uncontrolled. Smouldering is more likely in highly controlled air or moist material. Shavings can sometimes self-extinguish if too moist.

appendix g: smoke spreader design

Smoke Spreader design

The matrix shows the minimum number of holes required for a smoke spreader

Smoke pipe diameter (mm)

Sq. mm		50	60	70	80	90	100	120	130	140	150
		1964	2828	3849	5027	6363	7855	11311	13275	15396	17674
10mm	79	25	36	49	64	81	100	144	169	196	225
15mm	177	11	16	22	28	36	44	64	75	87	100
20mm	314	6	9	12	16	20	25	36	42	49	56
25mm	491	4	6	8	10	13	16	23	27	31	36

optimum number of holes required for a smoke spreader

Smoke pipe diameter (mm)

Sq. mm		50	60	70	80	90	100	120	130	140	150
		1964	2828	3849	5027	6363	7855	11311	13275	15396	17674
10mm	79	38	54	74	96	122	150	216	254	294	338
15mm	177	17	24	33	43	54	67	96	113	131	150
20mm	314	9	14	18	24	30	38	54	63	74	84
25mm	491	6	9	12	15	19	24	35	41	47	54

L I L I *food smoking*

appendix 2.
smoke-spreader design

appendix h: food hygiene guidance

colour-coded boards

Although it isn't currently a legal requirement in the UK, many commercial kitchens choose to use sets of colour-coded chopping boards to help prevent spreading germs from one food to another during food preparation. Different coloured boards are used for different types of food. The accepted colour-coding system in the UK is as follows.

Yellow: cooked meats
Red: uncooked meats
White: bread and dairy
Blue: raw fish
Green: fruit and salad
Brown: vegetables

Both plastic and wooden colour-coded boards are available. If you don't want to have this number of boards, try to keep a separate board for uncooked meats.

general chopping board hygiene

Regardless of what type of chopping board you choose, keep them hygienic by following these simple rules.

- never put ready-to-eat food on to a chopping board which has been used for preparing raw meat unless it has been thoroughly cleaned first
- always carefully scrape off pieces of food then wash the board in hot, soapy water or a dishwasher after use
- after you have washed it, spray the chopping board with a food-safe antibacterial spray
- if possible, store your chopping boards in an upright position - this allows the boards to dry more effectively than lying flat in a drawer or cupboard

appendix i: temperature conversion table

TEMPERATURE CONVERSION TABLE

°C	°F	°C	°F	°C	°F	°C	°F	°C	°F	°C	°F	°C	°F
-40	-40.0	-10	14.0	20	68.0	50	122.0	80	176.0	110	230.0	140	284.0
-39	-38.2	-9	15.8	21	69.8	51	123.8	81	177.8	111	231.8	141	285.8
-38	-36.4	-8	17.6	22	71.6	52	125.6	82	179.6	112	233.6	142	287.6
-37	-34.6	-7	19.4	23	73.4	53	127.4	83	181.4	113	235.4	143	289.4
-36	-32.8	-6	21.2	24	75.2	54	129.2	84	183.2	114	237.2	144	291.2
-35	-31.0	-5	23.0	25	77.0	55	131.0	85	185.0	115	239.0	145	293.0
-34	29.2	-4	24.8	26	78.8	56	132.8	86	186.8	116	240.8	146	294.8
-33	-27.4	-3	26.6	27	80.6	57	134.6	87	188.6	117	242.6	147	296.6
-32	-25.6	-2	28.4	28	82.4	58	136.4	88	190.4	118	244.4	148	298.4
-31	-23.8	-1	30.2	29	84.2	59	138.2	89	192.2	119	246.2	149	300.2
-30	-22.0	0	32.0	30	86.0	60	140.0	90	194.0	120	248.0	150	302.0
-29	-20.2	1	33.8	31	87.8	61	141.8	91	195.8	121	249.8	151	303.8
-28	-18.4	2	35.6	32	89.6	62	143.6	92	197.6	122	251.6	152	305.6
-27	-16.6	3	37.4	33	91.4	63	145.4	93	199.4	123	253.4	153	307.4
-26	-14.8	4	39.2	34	93.2	64	147.2	94	201.2	124	255.2	154	309.2
-25	-13.0	5	41.0	35	95.0	65	149.0	95	203.0	125	257.0	155	311.0
-24	-11.2	6	42.8	36	96.8	66	150.8	96	204.8	126	258.8	156	312.8
-23	-9.4	7	44.6	37	98.6	67	152.6	97	206.6	127	260.6	157	314.6
-22	-7.6	8	46.4	38	100.4	68	154.4	98	208.4	128	262.4	158	316.4
-21	-5.8	9	48.2	39	102.2	69	156.2	99	210.2	129	264.2	159	318.2
-20	-4.0	10	50.0	40	104.0	70	158.0	100	212.0	130	266.0	160	320.0
-19	-2.2	11	51.8	41	105.8	71	159.8	101	213.8	131	267.8	161	321.8
-18	-0.4	12	53.6	42	107.6	72	161.6	102	215.6	132	269.6	162	323.6
-17	1.4	13	55.4	43	109.4	73	163.4	103	217.4	133	271.4	163	325.4
-16	3.2	14	57.2	44	111.2	74	165.2	104	219.2	134	273.2	164	327.2
-15	5.0	15	59.0	45	113.0	75	167.0	105	221.0	135	275.0	165	329.0
-14	6.8	16	60.8	46	114.8	76	168.8	106	222.8	136	276.8	166	330.8
-13	8.6	17	62.6	47	116.6	77	170.6	107	224.6	137	278.6	167	332.6
-12	10.4	18	64.4	48	118.4	78	172.4	108	226.4	138	280.4	168	334.4
-11	12.2	19	66.2	49	120.2	79	174.2	109	228.2	139	282.2	169	336.2

appendix j: characteristics of wood for food smoking

The following list of smoking woods has been collated in the main through my own research and from the research of others. There is a general rule of thumb which holds water and it concerns some of the woods that are readily available but are not suitable for smoking. The rule is this: if the fruit from the tree can be eaten then it's likely we can use the wood for smoking food. Obviously in the case of oak we don't eat acorns but they are eaten by foraging animals and we have widely been using oak to smoke food for millennia. There are a few exceptions to the rule but generally I find it to be a pretty good yardstick to determine if it's safe to use a particular wood for food smoking. The key is: if in doubt don't smoke with it.

alder: very delicate smoke with a hint of sweetness. Good with fish, pork, poultry, and light-meat game birds. Traditionally used in the USA to smoke salmon and similar in aroma to sweet chestnut.
almond: a nutty and sweet smoke aroma, good with all meats. Difficult to source in the UK but almond shells work just as well.
apple: slightly sweet but heavier, fruity smoke aroma. Beef, poultry, game birds and pork (particularly ham and cheese).
apricot: the aroma is milder and sweeter than hickory. Good with most meats.
ash: fast burning wood, light but distinctive almost aromatic aroma. Good with fish and red meats.
beech: a wonderful traditional light smoke with a subtle light, sweet aroma that goes extremely well with bacon, hams, sausage and mild cheeses.
birch: medium hard wood with an aroma similar to maple. Good with pork and poultry.
cherry: slightly sweet, fruity smoke aroma. Good with all meats and particularly good with cold smoked salmon.
chestnut (sweet): slightly sweet, nutty aroma, plentiful in the UK. Good with most meats and a good substitute for alder.
grape vines: aromatic earthy quality, similar to fruit woods like apple and pear. Good with most meats and cheese.

hawthorn: an aromatic smoke with a hint of sweetness in its aroma. Good with game and red meats. In plentiful supply in UK hedgerows.

hazel: a light smoke with a unique aromatic aroma that works really well with light meats and fish. Plentiful in the UK, Europe and USA.

hickory: pungent, smoky, bacon-like aroma. The most common wood used in the US. Good for all smoking, especially pork and ribs. Available in the UK, mainly through DIY outlets, and heavily used in barbeque smoking.

lavender: a delicate, aromatic lightly-scented smoke good with white meat, chicken and fish.

lemon: Medium light smoke with a hint of citrus fruit aroma. Excellent with beef, pork and poultry.

lilac: very light, subtle with a hint of floral aroma. Good with seafood and lamb.

maple: Mild smoke, somewhat sweet aroma. Good with pork, poultry, cheese, vegetables and game. Very similar in character to sweet chestnut and slightly sweeter than alder.

mesquite: strong, robust, earthy aroma. Good with most meats, especially beef, pork, venison and most vegetables.

mulberry: mild sweet aroma similar in character to apple. Goes well with beef, poultry, game, pork (particularly ham).

nectarine: the aroma is milder and sweeter than hickory with a hint of citrus. Good with most meats and fish.

oak (white or English): one of the most popular and versatile wood smokes. Heavy tannin smoke aroma. Good with red meat, pork, fish (especially salmon) and heavy game. Good with cheese. Gives a good colour and flavour to food.

olive: the smoke aroma is similar to mesquite, but distinctly lighter. Delicious with beef veal or, poultry but hard to come by in the UK.

orange: medium smoke with a hint of sweetness in its aroma; excellent with beef, pork and poultry.

peach: slightly sweet, earthy aroma. Good with most meats and cheese.

pear: slightly sweet aroma similar in character to apple. Good with poultry, game, pork and cheese. Excellent with oily fish.

pecan: similar in character to hickory, but not as strong. Try smoking with the shells as well. Good for most red meats and pork.

plum: the aroma is milder and sweeter than hickory. Good with most meats.

rosemary (dried leaves or stems): this herb gives a wonderfully light aromatic aroma and can be used as a finish to smoked lamb, pork, fish or chicken.

walnut (English): very heavy smoke aroma, usually mixed with lighter fruit woods. Can be a little overpowering if used alone. Good with red meats and game. Even the shells can be used so don't throw them away.
whiskey oak: made from old whiskey casks the staves from these barrels give the traditional oak smoked flavour with the addition of a sweet caramelised note from the cask contents. Wonderful with pork, beef or chicken and can be used as a replacement for oak to give an additional flourish. Smoked salmon smoked in whiskey oak is sensational.

The vast majority of people who attend my food smoking courses find the difference in characteristics of the various wood smokes quite remarkable. Smoke for some producers appears to have become a generic ingredient in all but the most discerning restaurants or food halls. Those making a distinction between oak smoked or apple smoked get my wholehearted support as I think it is this distinction between the various characteristics of different woods that makes food smoking a complete voyage of discovery for those willing to experiment with different combinations of wood.

You don't need to use just one wood either. I like to demonstrate this by using a mild wood like beech to impart an underlying flavour and aroma to a particular food, then showing how it can benefit from a sprinkling of herb just at the end of smoking to add a characteristic aroma to the food.

A good example of this is the technique I use when hot smoking a lamb shoulder on the barbeque. To finish off the smoking I add a few rosemary sprigs to give some characteristic rosemary aroma to the lamb before resting and serving. Discovering that was a good afternoon's work even though I say so myself.

This technique is equally effective when cold smoking and can add a further dimension and complexity to your food.

resources

See www.lowimpact.org/smoking for lots of information, books, websites and food smoking courses all over the UK.

smoker suppliers and manufacturers

Most of these sites provide wood chips/dust for smoking and have some food smoking recipes too.

Arden Smokers' Supplies
c/o Outdoor Gourmet

3 Dean Court Farm
Lower Dean,
Buckfastleigh,
Devon, TQ11 0LT
www.foodsmoker.co.uk
01364 644965

Bradley Smoker
www.bradleysmoker.co.uk
01803 712712
Customer service line is open 9 am - 3pm, Monday to Friday

Brook's Home Smokers
Ivor Lodge
63 Lillington Road
Leamington Spa
CV32 6LF
www.brookshomesmokers.co.uk
01926 494260

For Food Smokers
28 New Road
Gomshall
Surrey GU5 9LZ
www.forfoodsmokers.co.uk
01483-550694

GardenXL
200 Brook Drive
Green Park
Reading
RG2 6UB
www.gardenxl.com/barbecues/fuel/food-smokers/cold
0118 923 0501

Grakka Ltd
4 Halwell Business Park
Halwell, Totnes
Devon, TQ9 7LQ
www.grakka.com
01803 712712
Suppliers of Bradley Smokers.

Hot Smoked
Wheatland Farm
Stoodleigh
Tiverton
Devon, EX16 9QE
www.hotsmoked.co.uk
01398 351604

Mac's BBQ
Unit 3A
Rosevear Rd Industrial Estate
Bugle
Cornwall PL26 8PJ
www.macsbbq.com
01726 851495

Old Smokehouse
1 High Street
Knaphill
Woking
Surrey GU21 2PG
www.the-old-smokehouse.co.uk
01932 841171

Outdoor Cook
Long Meadow
Priory Road
Forest Row
East Sussex RH18 5HP
www.outdoorcook.co.uk
01892 710747

SausageMaking.org
www.sausagemaking.org
0845 643 6915

Smokedust
www.smokedust.co.uk

Weschenfelder
2-4 North Road
Middlesbrough
TS2 1DD
www.weschenfelder.co.uk
01642 247524
Wood chips/dust for smoking.

West Country Cold Smoker
21 Creedy Road
Crediton
Devon, EX17 1EW
www.coldsmoker.com
01363 773557

information

Anisakis parasite
http://www.food.gov.uk/foodindustry/guidancenotes/hygguid/guidsalmonanisakis
Essential guidance for preparing smoked salmon safely.

Brinkmann
www.brinkmann.net/recipes.aspx
Smoking tips and recipes.

Country Skills for Modern Life
http://countryskillsblog.com/themes/smoking-and-curing-posts-including-diy-cold-smoker-build
Interesting blogs on smoking and curing.

Downsizer
http://www.downsizer.net/Articles/Cooking,_preserving_and_home_brewing/Filing_Cabinet_Hot%10Cold_smoker
How to build a smoker from a filing cabinet.

Food Standards Agency
www.eatwell.gov.uk
http://www.food.gov.uk/multimedia/pdfs/hygieneguidebooklet0310.pdf
http://www.food.gov.uk/multimedia/pdfs/foodhygieneguide.pdf
http://www.food.gov.uk/business-industry/caterers/sfbb/#.UdqD-fnCZQY
(Safer food, Better Business)

Foodsafety.gov
http://www.foodsafety.gov/keep/basics
US site for health and safety guidance about Clean, Separate, Cook and Chill.

Galloway Smokehouse
www.gallowaysmokehouse.co.uk/
Recipes and information on the smoking process.

the Gastronomic Gardener
www.gastronomicgardener.com/smoke-shack-build-cold-smoker-part-1
How to build a wooden 'smoke shack'.

the Guardian
www.theguardian.com/lifeandstyle/2010/apr/24/home-smoking-recipes-hugh-fearnley-whittingstall
home smoking recipes from Hugh Fearnley-Whittingstall.

National Center for Home Food Preservation
http://nchfp.uga.edu/how/cure_smoke.html
US site with lots of articles about smoking and curing various foods.

Oregon State University
www.lowimpact.org/smoking_fish.pdf
4-page pdf about smoking fish safely

Smoked Fish A-Z:
www.mexican-barbecue-recipes.com/smoked-fish.html
comprehensive guide to smoking fish

Smoking Pit
www.smokingpit.com/Info/How-to-Cold-Smoke-Meat-Nuts-cheese.htm
How to cold smoke meat, nuts and cheese.

Squidoo
http://arts-humanities.squidoo.com/how-to-build-smoker
great page on how to build various types of smoker, plus recipes

Storey Country Wisdom Bulletin
www.lowimpact.org/smokehouse.pdf
32-page pdf on how to build a smokehouse,

books

All the books below are available from
www.lowimpact.org/books_food_smoking.htm

Practical Food Smoking: a Comprehensive Guide
Kate Walker, 1995

Cold-Smoking and Salt-Curing Meat, Fish & Game
A D Livingston, 2010

The Smoking and Curing Book
Paul Peacock, 2007

Meat Smoking and Smokehouse Design
Stanley, Adam & Robert Marianski, 2009

Home Smoking and Curing: How to Smoke-Cure Meat, Fish and Game
Keith Erlandson, 2009

Self-Sufficiency - Home Smoking and Curing
Joanna Farrow, 2012

Made at Home: Curing and Smoking
Dick and James Strawbridge, 2012

A Guide to Canning, Freezing, Curing and Smoking Meat, Fish and Game
Wilbur F Eastman Jnr, 2002

Mastering the Craft of Smoking Food
Warren R Anderson, 2007

Get Smokin'
Cookshack, 2001

Charcuterie: the Craft of Salting, Smoking and Curing
Michael Ruhlman and Brian Polycyn, 2005

Smoking Food
Ricky Gribling, 1999

Smoking Food: a Beginner's Guide
Chris Dubbs and Dave Heberle, 2008

The Smoked Foods Cookbook: How to Flavour, Cure and Prepare Savoury Meats, Game, Fish, Nuts and Cheese
Lue and Ed Park, 1992

other LILI publications

Learn how to heat your space and water using a renewable, carbon-neutral resource – wood.
This book includes everything you need to know, from planning your system, choosing, sizing, installing and making a stove, chainsaw use, basic forestry, health and safety, chimneys, pellet and woodchip stoves The second edition has been expanded to reflect improvements in wood-fuelled appliances and the author's own recent experience of installing and using an automatic biomass system.

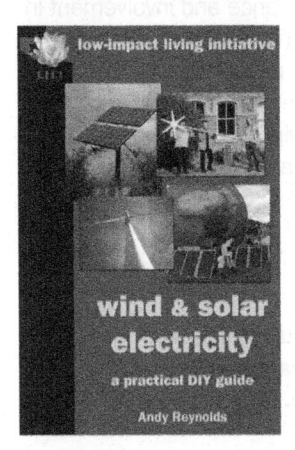

The author has been providing his own electricity from the sun and the wind for many years and in the first edition of wind and solar electricity he shared his knowledge and experience to explain how his readers could do the same.
Subsequent developments in the associated technology and UK government incentives have led him to make substantial revisions and additions to the original text, including new illustrations and photographs, for this second edition. He provides practical, hands-on advice on all aspects of setting up and keeping a home-generation system running and the text reflects his own recent experience.

The author grew up in Jamaica and was taught to make soaps by her grandmother. They grew all the plants they needed to scent and colour their soaps and even used wood ash from the stove to make caustic potash.
Her book is intended for beginners, includes both hot- and cold-process soap making, with careful step-by-step instructions, extensive bar, liquid and cream soap recipes, full details of equipment, a rebatching chapter plus information on the legislation and regulations for selling soap.
Now also available as part of an an online course at:
http://lowimpact.org/online_courses_natural_soaps.html

***how to spin: just about anything* is a wide-ranging introduction to an ancient craft which has very contemporary applications.**
It tells you all you need to know about the available tools, from hand spindles to spinning wheels, what to do to start spinning, with illustrated, step-by-step instructions, and a comprehensive guide to the many fibres you can use to make beautiful yarns.

Janet Renouf-Miller is a registered teacher with the Association of Weavers, Spinners and Dyers, and has taught at their renowned Summer School.

***solar hot water: choosing, fitting and using a system* provides detailed information about solar-heated water systems and is particularly applicable to domestic dwellings in the UK.**
Lee Rose has 10 years of experience and involvement in every aaspect of the solar thermal industry in the UK and around the world. His book provides a comprehensive introduction to every aspect of solar hot water: including all relevant equipment, components, system design and installation and even how to build your own solar panels.

Compost toilets reduce water usage, prevent pollution and produce fertiliser from a waste product. Built properly they can be attractive, family friendly and low maintenance.
This DIY guide contains everything you need to know about building a compost toilet, plus proprietary models, decomposition, pathogens and hygiene, use and maintenance, environmental benefits, troubleshooting and further resources.

186 food smoking **L I L I**

herbal remedies: how to make, use and grow them **teaches you to identify, grow and harvest medicinal plants.** It shows you how to make a range of simple medicines; there are sections on body systems, explaining which herbs are useful for a range of ailments, and detailed herb monographs. This second edition has been revised to take account of recent changes in UK legislation.

Sorrell Robbins is a highly-qualified, leading expert in natural health with over 15 years experience. She teaches at all levels from beginner to advanced postgraduate and is a regular contributor to many natural health publications.

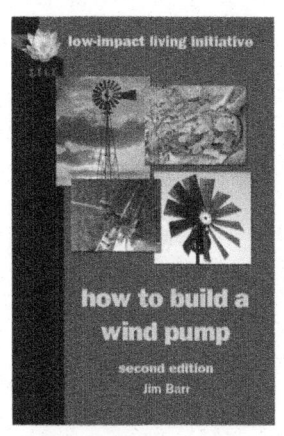

Good for developed or developing countries, the wind pump described in this book can pump rainwater, greywater, river, pond or well water for irrigation, aerate a fish pond, run a water feature or even be a bird scarer. This system does not generate electricity. The turbine is 700mm diameter and the turbine head plus rotor weighs less than 4kg. In a light-to-moderate wind it should pump about 1000 litres a day with a head of 4-5 metres. If you have good engineering skills and equipment you can fabricate nearly all of the system yourself; if you get all the parts manufactured, it's not much more complicated than DIY flatpack furniture.

This book contains 50 practical ideas for ways that you can help to stem the tide of destruction that is overtaking the ecology of our one-and-only planet. It's a random selection from the 170 topics on our website. Each chapter is a topic from one of the following five categories:
- shelter
- land
- lifestyle
- food & drink

Each topic is then divided into three sections:
- what is it?
- benefits
- what can I do?

notes

notes